'Enjoy the Revolution'

Sunny Jetsun

'Enjoy the Revolution'
Sunny Jetsun - Copyright 2015 by Sunny Jetsun
Createspace Edition   978-1-910363-21-8

This Anthology #1 also includes a selection of favourite
writings from all the books of Ciel Rose & Sunny Revareva
which were the previous pseudonyms of Sunny Jetsun.

Originally Published as Sunny Jetsun
'Driving My Scooter Through The Asteroid Field
Coming Down Over Venus ~ "Hallo Baba"
**'Light love Angels from Heaven. New Generation,
Inspiration, Revolution, Revelation ~
All the Colours of Cosmic Rainbows'**
'Green Eve * Don't lose the Light Vortex *
My brain's gone on holiday ~ free flowing feelings'
**'Surfing or Suffering ~ together * Sense Consciousness
fields of a body with streams and stars of hearts'**
"When You're happy you got wings on your back ~
Reposez vos oreilles a Goa; We're only one kiss away"
'PSYCHIC PSYCHEDELIC'
'Streaming Lemon Topaz Sunbeams'
'Invasion of Beauty *FLASH * The Love Mudras'
'Patchouli Showers ~ Tantric Temples'
'It's Just a Story ~ We Are All The Sun, Sweet Surrender'
Anthology # 2 ~ 'Love & Freedom ~ Welcome'
'He Lives in a Parallel Universe'
'Queen of Space ~ King of Flower Power ~ dripping Rainbows'
'All Love Frequency ~ In Zero Space'
*Peace Goddess*Spirit of the Field*The Intimacy Sutras*
**'Heavenly Bodies ~ Celestial Alignments*
Feeling ~ Energy that Is LOVE in Itself'**
'I've been to Venus & back*These Are Real Feelings*
Let the Universe Guide Your Heart*through Space'
*The Kiss In Slaughterhouse 6 *

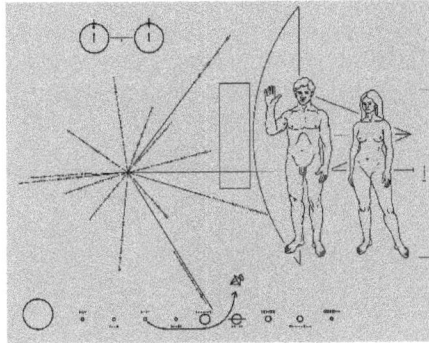

Books by the Same Author:

Originally Published as Ciel Rose
'Sadhu Sadhu Sadhu ~ "All Beings Be Happy" ~ Shanti Shanti'
'Trilogy Of Vibrations ~ The Oneness Of Life'
'Each Fragment of Life Is Sacred ~ These Are Your Children'
'Young Women Spin On Their Doorsteps At Dusk'
'Life Is Simple, Sharing ~ Loving Kindness From The Heart'
'The Universe Coming Across The River'

Originally Published as Sunny Revareva
'Pure Light ~ Cosmic * Sweet Heart ~ We've All Got Stars Inside'
'Perfect Love ~ No Mind * Star Light ~ Come Alive'
'True Freedom ~ Natural Spiritual Beauty ~
Here * Now ~ Gems of Eternity'

Sunny Jetsun Online at:
Website: www.sunnyjetsun.com
Facebook: www.facebook.com/sunnyjetsun
Amazon: www.amazon.com/author/sunnyjetsun
Smashwords: www.smashwords.com/profile/view/sunnyjetsun

Why Travel is an Ultimate Experience.
Outside Fixed Spheres ~ Universal Image
*

'The Frontiersman'
Always at the limit ~ the frontier
Word - symbol - for Frontier of your mind.
Frontier ~ At your limit
Always on the Point of Discovery.
To live is to be ~ In Infinite Discovery
Consciousness of the new moment
And New Limit
The Frontier to the next moment
Moment of Discovery
The Universe is Infinite ~ Discovery.
Living on the Frontier
Time is your Immediate ~ Environment
Now is the moment ~ Your Instant Adaptation.
Adaptation can be made Your Lifetime.
Adaptation is your end of your Frontier.
Static, your environment Lives on You
You are your environment ~ Your World
Now, Again, Now ~ Adaptation ~
You lose the sense of the Frontier
The limit to limitless
Sense of Discovery, Timeless ~
You are existing in a fixed world
It builds within its sphere
Time Is Inside ~ You are inside
Inside Time.
Outside Time is Infinity
You are Infinity
On the Frontier of Discovery of you
Instantly Forever

1

*Beauty in Heaven is
anything alive and
growing in Nepal.*

*

I'm doing
*whatever people like me do
around Kathmandu
just take 1kg. of good hash
and fly to Annapurna.
Take a trek to the meadows ~
of Rhododendrons
listen to her falling streams.*

*

Sujata
*'Superman or Tarzan'
I Love you Jane
bathing in a waterfall ~
Golden Parrots singing in the trees.
Red Riding Hood, Robin Hood or Buddha hood.
Great Compassion ~ nuclear alms.*

*

To Anicca ~ Anicca ~ Anicca
*Please don't miss isles ~
Silver porpoise, pastel flying fish.
Calmly watching each Instant
Changing ~ Buddha sky.
True Happiness, Taking the liner 'Meditation'
waves surf ~ the Sea of Moments
a new beginning*

*

*message to the animals, that we are coming,
coming in Peace. That we've got to come;
It will be cool and the animals responded.*

<u>Nature</u>
nature is the woods and the ocean
the trees and the cliffs ~
the fields and the meadows
the flowers and the seaweed
the hills and the plains and lakes
nature is the butterflies
and for all our sakes.
*

<u>The beautiful faces of happy children</u>
Pokhara valley ~ nature and humans.
Lake Phewa,
Gurung villages
The Annapurna range
Timelessness.
Tibetan traders, antiques, stones,
silver, ringing bowls, coral beads.
Turquoise, Rich local people.
Gold earrings, nose rings
the bazaar, tailors, chai,
people working, activity, life.
Amazingly beautiful women,
upright, proud, strong, desirable
carrying their water jars,
working so hard ~
washing in the lake.
*

<u>God is</u>
Alive and well and has
acquired an abode in Nepal
still his best friends
are living along ~
the Gulf of Siam

Paradise Heaven

I thought I was in heaven
setting of the Sun how bright.
What amazing Colours you spray.
Greens, yellows, all the amazing shades.
The turquoise, blue sea its current flows by ~
The Sun's white Golden beams reflecting
changing frequencies in the purple ripples.
My dimension is moving ~
What is real, am I alive or dead?
Dead in the Universe.

*

A sight of Heaven, as the Universe.
Can't look anymore ~ Gives
the feeling of strong movement
Crashing, reeling my brain.
The texture of the sand,
the tastes, the chills ~ horrible.
Yes but there is Heaven too.
Will I move again or am I real, just
a viewer, an eye on the Supreme reality;
Is it Supreme reality?
I'm still conscious
of the reality by which I arrived here.
This is Thailand isn't it?
This is a place? This beach, those trees,
the distant people, are they my imagery?
No they are real, so are you.
A trip, don't lose it.

*

'Inspiration' ~ doesn't always come easy
sometimes it takes a 22 hour bus ride.
Goa is my Meditation * connects me to the Universe

My darling who invites the spirits if they wish
to enjoy the strawberries and desert figs ~
so your caravan will glide to Kilimanjaro to
sing there and perform Kabuki for your Lord.
My darling
Ambrosia is the sweet juice
on your lips ~ wet
and between your legs,
Spirits at your side
desire so much your blossom
as a bee cherishes the perfume
of the sweetest flower
Subtle are their extractions
as they enter the soft petals
Inside they wish your sparkle
but today your colour has fallen pale
and your eyes gleam less.
The dazzle of your movements is slow, my darling
who has yet to sail by felucca down the Nile and to
meditate in quiet under the pinkest trees of mount Fuji.
My darling whose perfume will scent
the nature of many delicate impressions.
Now your sweetest strength of life
is needed to fountain many loves
and to warm erogenous twinkles
as you do now my heart and pupils.
Spirits fall as leaves to allow ~
the spring and summer of your sailing.
The bluest Oceans will yet see ~ your caravan
pass in wildest colour ~ to the golden dunes.
Spirits sit and drink with me ~ at the oasis
Purple nomads will feed us dates ~
Strength for the star route.

The throne of the Universe
is camouflaged on Earth
and has the name of
Everest
*

I think
Lou Reed produces the music
capturing the color full freaks,
the humorous, the silent, unknowing of
the "yeah man you digging it too" people.
Who were seen ~
in very dark restaurants in Amsterdam
and on top of volcanoes in Guatemala
sometimes ~ gathering after rain,
the Magic mushrooms
of Mexico & Bali, Indonesia.
*

The difference between
'Realty and Reality'
Is in the 'I'
Realty or Reality ~
'Realty Company Limited'
*

Travel
Buddha ~ the last Resort
Dear Sanctuary
Pure light
Deathless Dhamma
Blessed are you
the middle path to ~
the cottage of Sublime beauty.
Peaceful ~ Love ~ Creation

In* Dia ~

Why in the so called largest democracy
in this World are there so many, many CAPITALISTS,
big greedy Capitalists, medium Capitalists and
lots of little Capitalists, on their way?
Why in a so called land of Spirit ~
is there so little free will and respect?
Why must families live on 6 sq. ft.
of pavement, on a busy boulevard
in India's largest Capitalist Centre?
Why India do you allow your husbands,
sons, and brothers to gain by robbing
the Capitalist way, Why do you let them
rob you so you hide your heart?
Is it right that old men should run
with horses all day in order
for the spoilt children of the rich
to squeal with delight in the sun?
India, India. India, can there be
any love left in your soul
or did it all go into making coal
for the Barons at your inner circle
and cruel exploiters so numerous?
Why, Why, India
do you let your people be so poor
and smile and grin and be so fat
in smug conceit with your dominion?
You have no sense of shame or feeling
of disgrace instead you laugh,
the joke's on them, the human race!
Within your feudal myth full mind you feel
it's they who owe you a deal and let the feeble World think
that you have some rightful excuse ~ that being so Holy
it could not be otherwise. Don't make me laugh, India!

Class Energy
A wrist to crack?
Violence, 'non'
building the Taj Mahal ~
having my lunch on the river bank
as free as can be ~

*

Metta
this day
I was at the end
& so too shown
to the traveller's Rest,
the Inn of U Ba Khin.
Offering of light Refreshment
he served ~ the clear day
Vipassana sky, a new breath
a new path ~ approaching
the Dhamma way

*

'Stravinsky'
Would you rather see your child
Conducting an Orchestra or
Commanding a battalion?
'Strafing Sky'

*

'Sinism'
Indian Baby
mock a sin
mermaids

*

My We ed Thing
This Big Connection with nature ~
Agreed Not Greed ~ freed not need!

Enjoying the Sun by the Ocean
enjoying it to dreaming of the pacific isles ~
then I want to think of the Chile coup model.
(free the people from themselves)
The Cruelest destruction of life
in men, women and children.
What sort of soldiers are these?
What sort of soldiers are these?
Unbelievable mankind
spending so much time to destroy.
Creating Violence for the final destruction
going out on a bomb ~ sending their people
out on a screaming pain.
Who are they?
I don't want to even think ~ of the Cold War.
'American liberators' in Viet Nam model.
Whose children were frightened?
Whose children were melted?
Whose children were killed?
Whose brothers and sisters ~
Screamed and Screamed and Screamed?
Do you feel it more fitting for a human being
to go out of Life ~ as a melted scream in a cloud?
Or from a human vision ~

*

'Who'
~ do you know what a Boddhisattva is?

*

"We're tapping the Same Dance"
Where would I like to be sprinkled ~
by the infinite Ganges ~ river Chanters.
On the Winds of the Goddess Annapurna
and in the hollows of little green trolls.
Inside the hearts of Murdered Children.

9

'Sons & daughters'
Mother, Father, Lovers
having a child
children ~
a bouquet of fleurs.
Children,
petals opening
mother, father, Lovers,
having a child ~
Children of the World
Fertilising with truth
Love, blooming Spirit.
*

Jewel Meaning
light & heavy
*Simple * deep*
life continues ~
in our Children.
Once upon a time
there were animals
flowers & trees
& birds singing ~
*

Known ~ own
Know ~ now
Knew ~ new
*

'Party'
'bring someone you Love'
*Love ~ ve * Evol ~ ve*
*

SatSang
"I think I had a good heart attack"

Common question to a traveller (of 20 years)
<u>*Which is your favourite country?*</u>
I Love the Country of Pink Floyd
I Love the Country of Jacques Cousteau
I Love the Country of Smiling children
I Love the Country of Birds high in the trees
I love the Country of Botticelli
I Love the Country of
Colorful windmills turning
I Love the Country of
Marie by the blue French window
I Love the Country of Acid Jazz &Fantasy
I Love the Country of
Cockatoos dancing on a crystal piano
I Love the Country of
a white rhinoceros sky
I Love the Country of
a lake of shining tipis
I love the Country of truth.

*

<u>*Shade of pink*</u>
Silurian blue pink.
Mikado's parasol
filigreed fingers ~
reaching Outward
to the sky.
Inside the thatched pagoda
of a golden Spider Queen.
Silken touch
pendulous in air ~
waves of Peonies & Lotus
opened

'Sweet Amazement'
I talked Children!
It sounded like Parrot
I don't know Gorilla
I've only seen dolphin
& I'm just now ~
getting to know kitten
& the magic silence
of birds
in the twilight Ocean!
*
Looking out my window
is like looking into an aquarium
the Sky is like the Sea
the birds are like the fish
a kitten is like a Green tropical plant
music is like the breeze
a Loving thought is like a pyramid
a loving act is like day & night
*
Collapse
I Looked onto a hillside reaching to the sea of
Parrot's wing and saw blue swimming pools
exactly situated on the terasse, a cocktail and
reservation on Air France to make a Safari.
The Coast was Complete with this quality
of Sophistication and desire. It was so
attractive to imagine such pleasures with you.
I Looked across the street from the plage and
saw a gypsy camp, it was raining and not
the Season to play, it made me think of
the Italian Lady struggling on the train
carrying her house

I am a hunter.
I Live by what I catch,
by putting it back once
having been nourished by it.
I am a hunter of dreams, catching so many
and riding them through the time of
my life. I am a hunter of hearts,
drinking their beads as Tiger scent.
I am a hunter of Universe's joy
after the Astral serpent's kiss ~
I am a hunter, a guest at your table
beloved host. I am a hunter, my
Grandfather is collecting Red tulips
in the snow. I am a hunter with
ancient codes tracking the game
over the Seven seas. I am a hunter from
dawn to dusk to meet you face to face.
I am a hunter my sweet child
*

To Chopin's Greatest Hits
He used to Love
a fashion model
from Paris, France
who grew up with
the best of the Republic.
Now
He's more than happy
when a kitten comes
to be stroked awhile
*

Meditation is like ~
Feeding the Birds.
Each Day

Karma 1

There's no such thing as a holy Renault
There's no such thing as a holy house
that needs a Lock to keep away the Ghost.
Your dreams can sink in minutes
with the eternal change ~
that is so subtle yet strikes when the time
is right for it. A Surging jet sound in the sky
that one day could say that you will die in 3 seconds.
There's no such thing as a holy Renault ~ it will sink
to the bottom of a river but you may still swim.
Give me the kiss that Unlocks the door
not the one that locks me in.

*

Goldfinch

Hanging from my Parachute.
Inside a great Banyan tree
my camouflage suit ~
hides my sight ~ from
a python of the night.
Beauty passes oh so near ~
to this nutmeg grove of fear.
For the warriors of this tribe
the Sun has set long ago ~
just the Rhythm of the stream
& magic force of dream.
Pastel Angels come to ease my pain ~
How long before they find the wreckage
& rest me in the land of herbs
& children's smiles ~
The branch is breaking
I'm on the ground
I hear a waterfall ~ sound

U

...Just a part of it ~ going around
(danger) praying for an answer, Becoming
~ Time ~ by you ~ river ~ exhausted ~
A GREENHOUSE FOR MY SEEDS OF SCHIZOPHRENIA
(latent) by you (a Karmic Lover) happens.
Cloudbursts in the abdomen, freaking out, disconnection.
Fearful Octopus, raging dogs, sharks, wriggling Serpents,
howling at the moon dear.
Dark ~ angel 'Transmissions!'

*

How do I get Wisdom ~
From where do I get Wisdom
Father
How do I get Wisdom
From where do I get Wisdom
Mother
'It's ok to die'

*

'Vol au vent'
I am at the root of ~
Intensity or ethereal
evaporating rapidly
Infinite relaxation.
Silver Samovar
& reindeer milk

*

Star
I feel as alone as one can feel.
Milarepa...'The Widow's mite'
'Pronoia' ~ The sneaking suspicion
that Someone ~ Is Conspiring
to help you!

<u>Listen: 5000 ethereal children singing to us</u>
Bright and early, 8.15 Summer holiday time, August 6th saw a
pink ball falling through the sky, then black, black whipping rain.
A moment, spontaneous, fantastic multi ~ coloured clouds.
Bright and early came the host of Death to live in the bodies
of 90,000 in sinner rated survivors, came the Enola Gay with
a genocidal mushroom of deadly destruction. A deadly gift to
all your children, free from US to your soul. Radiation, gamma
rays, diseases to explode you into a heap of melted hearts ~
charred bones of a beautiful girl and wheelbarrows of shadows.
Your mother melted into stone; A great collection for your
prayers of peace, peace! 18 hundred feet, 10 thousand miles
from home, "bombs away!" All life turned to ash, flower ash,
grandfather ash, tree ash, eye ash, skin ash, sister ash, brother
ash, mother ash, dad ash. So many years of your hell standing
in the ruins; B29 turns. A Flying fortress swings to its home ~
Sayonara. Full of surprises! Did you know there were 20,000
women pregnant with tomorrow? Did you know about the
children who fold paper cranes now and float paper lanterns
in the Toronagashi festival to hold a little longer their spirits?
It all happened too quickly ~ you were gone, evaporated!
I never had a moment to say goodbye to you my child.

*

<u>Toi ~ Gallia</u>
You Are the smell of a damp forest
You Are the taste of the azur sea ~
You Are the touch of a Mercy full Angel
You are the Sight of forever & ever
Vous etes les sons d'amour

*

"We decided that our Indian
People Are More Important
to us than long jail terms"

"Your Mother Was a Painter"
Ghee in my heart
Ghee in my brain
Ghee in my toes
Ghee in my fingers
Ghee in my knees
Sweet Surrender
Unique ~ Unique.
House in the Camarque
beside you ~ at dawn.
Your Mother was a Poetess
*

Unique
Now ~ by a palm tree grove ~
Your father was a Fisherman.
Your Father was a Pearl diver.
He would sit for your mother ~
Already a bright tropical 5am.
Vases of wild flowers ~ soft breeze.
Sound of the Crashing Surf.
Precious ~ Times ~ There.
*

'daughter'
Viking ship ~
Seeking ~ a new passage
Standing alone on the bow
Stars ~ of my village
****

Softly treads the Paris sky
I'm in your Country
but you don't know
Long legged enchantress ~
Morning's ~ early Autumn beauty

"FRIJOLES 0 FUSILES POLICY" *
1978-1983, At least ~ 12,000 Unarmed
Civilians have DIED... BY VIOLENCE
In Guatemala. (Amnesty International).
The Music of the guitar strings
has gone dead.
Throughout the Mountains.....at night.
*

'Guatemalan Bells'
"With a Member stuffed in his Mouth"
"Who has found my Lover...?"
Who are these Peanut Advisors
Cultivating terror>>::<<Genocide?
And the World pleads....Ignorance!!
When Helicopters Come
they Come to Massacre
Our families.
*

'Killers of a Trained Army'
As for My Family...They Killed Seven
Chopped them up with Machetes
They are the 'Kaibiles'
Guatemalan 'Special Forces' Si Si Si:
Mr. President.
*

Aiding In ~ Guatemalan Cemeteries!
A Government of Death. Tyrants, despotic.
Who Is Supporting You Mr. Totalitarian President?
Nothing Can Convey....The Army's Mutilation.
"As of My family They Killed Seven"
Hacking - My Family ~ To Pieces.
My Family ~ To Pieces!
'Education'

Patrol The Election
We Are Another Democracy?
Si...just as you wish Emperor.
Brutality of Its Leaders
Brutality of Its Leaders.
Poor Peasants.
Soldiers On Guard...Guarding.
Fighting for your Existence
Against <> This Brutality.
*

Do you know how much Aid is Given
from America to this Fascist Government?
Devil In the Mirror ~ OLIGARCH, WHY?
Smashing the fruit ~ cutting the cane.
I found my family burning in Pieces.
Army Cremating's.
*

'Outside US'
COMMUNITY LEADER ~ COMMUNITY,
Testimony. Kidnapped by 'Unknowns'
His decapitated body was Dumped
in Front of the neighbourhood School.
A Project he had Supported ~
Whirring grief
*

'What do All the People Say About this?
What do you say..
"Que tal amigo?"
What do you do.....Human Kind?
Meanwhile a new helicopter ~ Armed arrives!
Presented to the Local Military Commander.
The history of Bombs, Your Excellency

(The Vatican has full diplomatic Relations with US!)
Do you Support the Resistance of this horror?
Manipulation of Superpower strings
for Sociopathic Neo Fascists.
The People are Suffering terribly

*

Those With the Government are Fed....
Those not with the Government are Shot.
All the Dancers are Missing
Dead and buried Where?
"We've exterminated All the Indians in
our Federal Republic, Mr. President!"
"What did you See Father Hennessey?"
"A prayer too horrible for words"

*

Where have all the Weavers gone?
Army Cadets learnt to Identify 'huipiles'
(traditional woven blouses)
by their Village of Origin.
'The Poly Technic Institute of Guatemala'
Conducting a Course In Murder on Indigenous
Cultures! Mr. President, Members of the Senate.
"How can we explain these terrorists?"
'Rainbow Coloured Folk'

*

'American Express'
Model used throughout the World.
Recognising, another False Flag strategy.
Needing an excuse to send in their mercenaries
to exploit & control it all ~ 'Family Massacre Sites'
Is this Development from the Developed!?
Don't you hold someone Responsible

for this Mr. Presidente?
They Shot All Our Weavers
And Burnt Them In 'Standard Oil'
Inventories/Who Counts?
"Another Family Massacre Site"
Your own Country Is Full of them...
Do you remember Wounded Knee,
Peace River, Dakota and Mai Lai?
*

'Guatemala City Morgue'
Equipped Army
"Our Equipped Army!"
Securing An Election
(Good Ratings, spinning the Media)
The funeral of Two peasants
dead Silence ~
pass the mourners.
Teaching Army Cadets
how to site a rocket on a peasant's blouse.
Heirs ~ There is a lot more
to a Loom than Meets the eye.
*

Congress Of...
Lies Lies Lies Lies Lies.
Deceit Lies In State ~ Understand!
We Massacre ~ Everything!
Don't Believe Anything Else.
(What do the Channels have to say?)
(What do the Gallop Polls predict?)
(What do the Figures demonstrate?)
(What do the Professionals think?)

21

Did the Kremlin send a wreath for each
Campesino ~ Is that what you Believe?
There is no risk for your Investments here
Uncle Sam, We understand very well
what you really want from us...&
We have created a special climate.
Monopoly of OLIGARCHY for you.
(US Power, 1954 was a great year
in Guatemala don't forget Senator)
*

Will you never Learn?
Cutting your Own throat
by Murdering humanity.
Food line ~ made elections in a famine.
For your vote you can eat our Democrazy!
This Machine - Gun (from good ol' USA)
Will Kill You & more ~
All your Loved ones too!
Refugees Surrounded
by a 'Muy Brutal Army'
Re Located to another ~
(Crazy Horse Reservation)
*

'US Greed Capital'
For your paper Dollari
we will condone anything
You Want
America!
Do you Want an Indian
Mutilated?
Playing the Gringo again Por Favor.
"We want to Grow very rich like you"
Teach US $$$$$$$$!

1983 Never Forget it!
A house where Women and Children
were burned to death ~ by the Army.
Nationalist Government Tactic! Si Si.
We Learn very well, Si?
Widowed Mother in....
Internal Refugee Camp...
Army Occupation....
Women most of them widowed
making Terraces ~
under Army's 'Food For Work' Program!
(Good for the Ratings...to lobby for more Aid)
Is that the country of the Quetzal
that was once so proud?
You didn't take long to destroy ~
but it will take more than forever to heal.
*

'Majority'
Fields abandoned
houses burned down
Looms destroyed
Army Visitation.
"We fled to the Forest."
A few managed
to get outside ~ the Country.
Many More Fight For Freedom.
*

'US Embassy Agenda'
New Imperial Officials ~ Ambassadors.
What's it feel like to be a Representative?
Travelling Salesman, Economic Hitmen.
Travelling Doom Merchant.
Oh to be an Apocalyptic Democraut!

God is on Your side, Right ~
then Why do you play the Devil?
Found only ten People left ~
You don't want any People left
No Looms ~ No Cornfields.
"You take away Our SPIRIT"
There is no SPIRIT left ~
You pressed it out of the People.
For a Life of Esclave age...
COMPRENDEZ.

*

U.N. Charter Is Where?
In any Place they Find us
They Kill us.
"As of My family ~
They Killed Seven.
Cut off their heads
Cut off their arms
their feet, hands."
"I am 10 years old"
Los Soldados ~
Nightmares in Red.
Violence Coming!

*

"They Hunted us like animals"
tells an old Guatemalan man.
Troops Killed ~ his Wife &
the Wife of his Grandson!
"I guess the Government does not
want anymore ~ Indian race"
Burned Our Fields.
Interview with refugee child....
"Cut off their organs" Commander!

'Whose Camp'
The Refugees had Already
started a Second Cemetery
for Many Children.
Grandfather with dead Grandchild
whose Parents had been Killed
by the army In Guatemala.

*

'We don't Want to Kill People'
The Army Is Obliging people ~
to burn their houses. If we do not
They Kill Us!
We are not in Agreement
to burn Our brothers' houses.
"Beat the guerrillas to death"
they say..."or we will Kill you"
"But We Are Not Criminals"

*

"Weavers of St. Sebastian"
The Soldiers Came
and seized 3 of us.
Killed them with Knives & Machetes!
Gathering Spilled Corn

*

Human Solidarity
Human Kind ~
And Who will Gain
with the Loss ~ of these PEOPLE
from their traditional land?
'BANG!'

*

** Arranged from: 'A Testimonial' Camera Work, London.
January 1984. Jean Marie Simon, 'Guatemala'

Stars Inside
gone to Heaven
after you.
I gave her a diamond
*

Galileo
Pentagon <> Vatican Truth.
Destruction of a body.
Forbidden fruit ~
'Know Your Enemy'
*

His heart had been broken!
A Lakota Sioux ~
They'd killed his brother.
Dead, had a family of 7
3 boys and 4 girls!
He gave me all that was left.
*

East Side
Passing the Buddhist Mission
peeking into ~ Tai Chi in action,
slowly twilight. A man parked
in a wheelchair asked kindly,
if I would like a cigarette?
"Thanks, what's your name?" "Dick"
I Promised him a book of poems.
Next time we meet.
*

Goa Freaks
Less Labels, less boxes, less Identities.
Into a new dimension ~ the Source Tao.
Getting rid of all the Conditioning ~
of the ego, chance to Observe, be Alive

Plato
Do they say ~
"It's Higher Karma
if you're Unemployed?"
Socrates had something
to say about Kings.
They put him to death
didn't they?

*

Surf Hotel
Un homme et une femme
Lands ~ of the Mind.
Beach peaches
and greedy man's need.
"Forgive me daughter"
dans moi ~
tu es une ange

*

L'Amandier
"Thus Have I Heard" She means business!
But she's got a heart ~ of Gold.
Sleeping in power points
honest support……
not an Exile ~ but a Hopi.
"Thus have I heard"
'A still mind, like still water,
yields a still reflection
of what is before it.'

*

'Turquoise dream'
Sun tanned ~ Women
Bringing out their Beautiful colours.
Divine

Greek Wisdom
Desires of a river
notes in your eyes
telepathy ~

*

'Arunta'
As you pass ~ over the land into
the dream ~ time of the Ancestors.
Between Consciousness & Matter
Psycho ~ historical map
of the 'Culture' ~ Yang loving Yin.

*

Redon Revival
"What did I put in my works that suggests
to them so much subtlety? I put in a little
door that was open on to mystery."
'A Soi Meme'

*

Something alive ~
Coming Out of the dark
Do not be afraid
INSIDE BEAUTY FEELING
FEELING IT
Sowing seeds ~ Who is Not a Slave?
"Interdependent in all its parts"
She gave ~
The Invader
Lavender
She gave ~
The Invader
Yellow Violets.
The Body Is Willing
so is the heart.

The Universe
Coming Across
The River
*

<u>*Yasodhara*</u>
Understanding with Compassion
forgiveness that gets rid of guilt.
It's forgiveness from the Heart ~
that gets rid of guilt in the Heart.
*

<u>*GB*</u>
They blew ~ the whole thing
with TV. over there!
Saxon's night out.
Arrows
*

<u>*Paradise*</u>
'The Monastery Highest'
Love.
I'm glad I came
Ahimsa.
*

<u>*'Katra'*</u>
Be Mind full of 'Changing' ~
no disturbance of thoughts arising.
Happiness is beyond feeling ~
together feeling for each other.
Cannot but share each other
Waves of Amour ~
MAKING LOVE.
MAKING ~ LOVE WITH YOU.
Temple of Aphrodite.
A Visit ~ With You

'Poetry is not merely an art of expression
but a Spiritual discipline'
*

In natural beauty
Loving to play ~
Against all the Insanity
of the World
Cosmic Truth of Tropical fish
Swimming ~
*

being there
Awareness
of the plumed serpent
eating a mango ~
afternoon Truth
*

Bright
moving On
with the Sun
Chaos of night
rain on the train
Horizon alight.
Smile
*

Festival of
performing costumes
letting go power ~
Clean & clear
typhoons
Singing

be ~
Cool generations

Peace * Love
flower garden
of Insight
*

Tangerine
the gathering of the tribes
materialises out of the blue
& into the light.
Lysergic storm troopers ~ Leary, Owsley,
Kesey, the Diggers, plenty of experience
of Alternative States.
*

Perfect Combination ~ Lotus Pond
"Turn On, Tune In, drop Out ~"
be awareness of the Life ~ stream.
Love ~ compassion ~ joy ~ equanimity
*

(Being ~ Occupied)
The 'Weeping Woman' Portraits seen from Parallel Universes.
Made a sketch of her being ravaged by a Minotaur in full heat!
Having respect for your compagnone, beside you through a War;
Whilst being motivated to paint Nazi aerial bombing; Genocide!
Holding your hand, being your Mistress, being your friend too.
Did you forget so easily ~ your sacred Muse?
*

'Switching on Your Tree of Light'
'Love is all around' ~ Depends how close you are to yourself!
Something's going on, play of energies, synergies, let's see.
"What's she doin'?" " ~ gettin' stoned & gettin' laid!"
"You would Not say No"
"I chased her out the Ward"
You gotta be Strong to Survive there.
Balance Problem

River of Life
Making Love to my Mind.
Water colours in Autumn
Then ~ Swept over a Waterfall
& mystery

*

Shoji
Listening to blossoms falling ~
and rocks growing your 'Wa' harmonies
messages to your centre "Sayonara Hara"
Please excuse my asking for Enlightenment.
Conscience less Culture, no sense of sin!
Quiet Sunset lights her obi.
Listening to the blossoms falling
letting Karma please itself
be innermost source with nature
No blinding Mind ~ no ugly.
No immeasurable pain from loss Lover.
Energy behind the Temples ~ Ineffable
not mere annihilation or nothingness.
Outside laws of causes & effects ~
this permanent Supramundane hara-gei.
Quiet Sunset lights her obi.

*

Mozart
Streams ~ of Winter Snow
Emerging, from below the ridge.
Afternoon ~ discoveries.

*

INASMUCHAS
'Sign of a wealthy personage
Life is what you can afford'
to Live with ~

Attack of Love
RIOT of COLOUR
LIGHT TO LIGHT
***

She was Founded by a Famous tea master
Composing gardens and pavilions
harmony of moss
raked ~ the Sense of Sublime Peace
*

Pure White Gold
Radiant Star of Energy.
Frangipani was the smell of all my Lovers,
feeling luscious ~ sexy Chromosomes.
Simply phenomena......
Life is a Tiger's eye Shark
Life is a King Cobra's mate.
Life is a thank you friend for giving
'A birth without violence'
Life is a desire to touch ~
Suffering is the same in any language.
Life is the same in any language.
Sensualness ~ "You left and found karate,
I became a Buddhist dearest."
On the middle path
*

'lese majesty'
'Less on ~ Jubilee'
Jubilation Where is the Liberty?
Equality No less.
Nothing less than 'Lese'
Lest accepting things that don't suit us!
'Mad Cows & Englishmen ~
Go Out In The Noon Day Sun'

Tender
Song of Intuition
Wonder of a Buddha.
Dear father ~ I Love walking
barefoot with you
thru an Indian Summer's Seaside Village.
A long, long road ~ maturing priestess.
Noble Silence's pearls of Wisdom.
A one room school house.
Truth is so beautiful

*

'Illumines'
Where are You Now
Where Will you be
April ~ Showers

*

Graciously
'London College of Art & Design'
.....Working by the Master
Mona Lisa brought wild flowers,
~ dawn
'The City University's MBA'
...sitting, listening to the Master's Metta
Liberates the Heart,
early this morning ~ peacefulness
'The Propaganda Machine'
......quietly accepting Dhamma
from by the river ~ Compassion

*

Sons & daughters
"Jesus
In the eyes of the Law
You Are Guilty!"

<u>Giving Amnesty</u>
Help ~ 'Liberate The Queen'
'Liberate The Royal Family'
'Liberate The Pope'
'Politicians'
Political Prisoners
On Your behalf!?
Their 'HUMAN' Rights Denied.
Strategy for a Political Objective!
'Liberate them from an Undemocratic Imposition'
Liberate them from their own Self's Injustice:
'their God-given rights' ~ to have Human Equality:
to speak freely, to think freely, to act freely,
taken away in the name of some False
'Democratic' duty! Is it really True?
Figure Heads hung in gilded cages.
Let them go ~
& let us go too
FREE
*

<u>'Magic'</u>
When You Lose Something
Precious
Give Something
Precious
to Someone true
Sojourns ~
*

<u>Healing</u>
Shattered wing ~ mirrors.
*

"AS IS WHERE IS"
"AS IT IS, SO IT IS OBSERVED
AND UNDERSTOOD"

'Heritage Cornucopia!'
They left us fields ~
with barb wire fences!
My friends
Enjoy the warm sunshine
in a valley, green, filled with
sacred lotus flowers, exotic birds,
waterfalls, lush plants, blue sky,
full of lovely dancing butterflies.
They left us fields ~
with Nuclear power sites!
My friends & children
Enjoy the waves ~
lapping on pebbled beaches, peacefulness,
the Magnificence of a Giant canyon ~ vista,
feeling warm turquoise waters, tranquil oasis.
They left us fields ~
Scattered with carcasses of poisoned industry.
My friends & family
Enjoy a quiet place ~
Inspired by stars so crystal bright,
good Psytrance music and Experiences.
Cool, happy, tuned in spiritual travellers,
sailing here by a full Moon for celebrating
these fantastic jewels of Earth's ~ beauty.
"How can you buy or sell the sky?"

*

Sheep
Is there any reason a fertile field
shouldn't be on an angle?
Whisper of ferns ~
Vincent's Cornfield, swaying
Meditation

Yoga Is 'No Ego', in Practice our divine destiny ~
In this context it is hoped to Show the complete negative
value of Propaganda, the reasons why it is used so fully
and who it benefits and why. From the description of the
Human Spirit it shows that Propaganda in fact Isolates,
alienates us from our own Self realisation and from the
Consciousness that we are a part of this Cosmic energy;
which is alive in everything, in the Natural Union 'Yoga'
~ of Life and reality. This Knowledge through Wisdom
helps us realise the True value of Life and the Untruth
of the Negative values described in 'Propaganda'
How are we to become connected to this Wise Sense of
'Our Universal Omnipresent Self' within the Globalised
perspectives of today? This is the future, with No fears.
Seen in meditation, poetry, Free Will, empathy, Creativity,
mystical vision, deep wisdom and Love, not the Propaganda
of fascism & racism 'Fundamentalism' of corrupted Despots,
tyrannical Politicians, Greedy Business, Media, Advertising
Moguls, Militarists and the Terror arising by mad extremists!
This development of Ignorance & Selfish manipulation of our
'Humanity' is an Attack on All of our Spiritual Realisations ~
Moments of Reality which for all of us are Changing essence.
All One, always flowing on ~ Our Ego is Not In Control of it.
Surrender and Transcend the Mind to eternal Boundlessness.
Don't get Attached but be Immersed with the Cosmic Stream ~
Timelessness, emptiness, silence with Source; Not Projections
by Ego's light. Walk the Pathless, True Path until you become
blissful Ocean, Sat Chit Ananda, Nibbana, love, Life, infinity ~

*

Arrangement of Homage to Solara
'The spirit experiences the world of form and limitation
in order to evolve itself back into Conscious Union
with that original oneness'

'Noa Noa' ~ Paul Gauguin
"Civilisation is falling from me little by little. I am
beginning to think simply, to feel only very little hatred
for my neighbour ~ rather to Love him. All the joys
animal and human, of a free life are mine. I have
escaped everything that is artificial, conventional,
customary. I am entering into the Truth, into nature.
Having the certitude of a succession of days like this one,
equally free and beautiful, peace descends on me. I develop
normally and no longer occupy myself with useless vanities."

*

No More 'WMD' "Words of Mass Deception!"
Eluded: He's A 'Real War Criminal Against Humanity!'
Not Imaginary vision, 'can't tell you what it's about but
got everything in it.' Shaman knowing how to use them
but Unfortunately Sectioned, banged up back home in UK!
'The Biggest Conspiracy Is our own Mind.' Sensitivity ~
This Understanding, Your connection, Your own Truth.
Honey Person, roots integrating to Earth Grand Mother.
Your Identifying with ~ So how far away from the Source?
Want too much for Ourselves; Liberation, Enlightenment
not the Ego Magic ~ use it wisely brother, sister, let it go.
'Means to an End' connected to Each Other in the flow ~
Everything sits on rhythms ~ more focused, not flipped out.
Contagious Inspiration in open fields of cosmic frequencies.
Speaking from the heart ~ sharing Unconditional Love

*

Pulling the Perjury Trigger
Feeling The Mind Wired Firing on me!
All going off at once. Exploding shooting stars
Feelings, Desires of a multi ~ Orgasm in you
all going off at once ~ her Celestial pulse sings.
Speaking in codes, sensations lighting synapses

True Existence of Reality

I said, "I gave my Promise ~ I Keep My Word."
'Propaganda' The Spell, certain types of Enchantment,
Transfixed, taking Possession of all your Spirits.
Webs of Black magic, Mesmerized, hypnotized,
Brain Washedise ~ Propagandised, Your being,
Possessed by, Done for a reason, the purpose to
Control. Needs the patient act of Understanding and
Rejection>< Attention!! Real Attention to Illusion
of Delusion. Fascinated by its powerful Magnetism,
Afraid of Fear! Weaknesses and dishonour, shame,
disgrace and guilt. Failed to undo the Spell of ~
Ignorance, greed, Selfish Ego, desire of possessing.
Who needs suffering & pain in such a debasing way?
What is the combination to this labyrinth of Illusion
devouring you? Entrapped; Belonging to Whom?
This karma of the Possessors, 'Being the Possessed'
Returning to Awareness back to Holistic Recognitions.
Propaganda has only Negative powers and vibrations;
Absolutely No human, Empathetic, Spiritual Qualities.
Remember Reality, of No Propaganda,
Demands Always ~ Truth Is Truth.
Not Tragic resignation ~
even from a broken heart

*

Dysfunctional Cock Up ~ You Live & Learn

Clean Screen light headed no screaming.
Wipe it, Swipe it, Brain wave ~ Washing.
What's your Branding ~ of deter gent?
Your Mind isn't that kind. 'Desert Storm'
Grains of plutonium ~ sand microbes imbibe.
Isn't that another War Crime, tell the Truth

A Sylph from Sybaris
'You can't have 'NO' ~ a duality in your heart'
Living Zero Point ~ 'Keep on Keepin' on'
ALL IN THE ONENESS
Never give up she's too beautiful.
"To tell you the truth brother."
Babble Babble avoid the rabble.
"Home is where you make it"~
Not where you're Not making it"
Apparently 'back in the day' ....when!
We need a Resolution. We need closure.
No propositions ~ the outlook is positive.
"Life is a Garden of delights"
"Love It"
*

'Targeted Disappoint ~ Meant'
'In order to know the true Union Consciously ~
we must experience the Illusion of Separation'
What's 'Expectation's Opposite'? 'No Expectation'
If you don't go there in the first place ~ detached,
can't be disappointed, does this make any sense?
"Don't do Anything with Craving Expectation"
Heart of Siddhartha Gotama, Heart of Buddha
Heart of Life, Heart of a good person, human being.
Here in the here and Now ~ respecting the cow.
Yeah, I can see your wings Angel ~ Essence
The Ultimate Trip, Giving*Birth ~ energies.
Spiritual dimensions ~ "Please Pick me!"
'Sat Chit Ananda' 'Om Mani Padma Hum'
Inspirational Compassion, Universal Being.
Love of a Mother from the Open heart ~
Coming up from the Sacred womb.
Pure Joy, No tragic, Pure Magic

LET'S GO WITH LOVE

Creating within your Self * Space
for Supra dimensional light Radiations.
No time to waste ~ No flame to waste
on Anger, greed, confusion, self indulgence, fear,
egocentric self delusion, or frequencies of disease.
True self on the Spiral ~ turning, Reawakening *
Look within Yourself, 'of the World Not In the World'
Agreement to go Thru Turmoil and difficulties
as an Altruistic Sacrifice for Higher purposes ~
To serve ~ brings glimpses of 'Cosmic Memory'
Open Your eyes Open your heart Open your Mind
Open your true Conscious Open our Divine Love.
Raising ourselves and the Plane's Vibration ~
to Higher Consciousness ~ 5th Dimension of Spirit.
Crystalline multi dimensional beings, Lovingly accept
Ourselves ~ End our Denial and Guilt trips, Merge ~
into the Highest Octave, possible thru simply ~ being.
Illuminating All with Deep Joy and Profound Peace.
"Because We Care"

*

Nibbana Om Jhana Banana

Foc*us Para ^ dime shift, Art balances ~
& codes of Abstraction in dhamma star seeds.
Radiant galactic rays, light fields to fulfill your days
& nights in your trips to Golden shimmering pyramids,
Emerald forests, Turquoise seas, Sacred Celebrations.
Embrace Open hearts divine Roller Coaster ~
Spirit * time dimension energy, Intuitive belief IS Real.
Opening your eyes through the bounteous Highest Chakra.
Mantra "Always lookin' on the bright side of life, do do."
'Sai Baba's message, 'Love All and be kind to All
Because I live & exist in All'

Sujata's Junket
The compassion of the Great Renunciation
'Subdue the body, set the Mind free ~
to Liberation' Found to be untrue. Abundantly
Clear, close to death not Enlightenment, Nibbana!
"May your aspirations be crowned with success"
By a Bodhi tree on the banks of Neranjara at Gaya.
No more becoming, end of all cravings, distortions ~
aversions, delusions, illusions. Her natural inspiration.
Great healer, embodiment of compassion and wisdom.
No more Bondage, but Self realization ~ Self Awareness
done by oneself, purifying the Mind to float Cosmically.
"born in the World as a lotus in the water * grew up,
lives in the world ~ has transcended the world
and lives Untouched by the World"

*

'Of the World But not In the World'
Motive to be Spiritual, practice non-materialism
Ideal. The Annunciation of Love and Compassion
Not Propaganda but Truth, that which is Real,
'My own experience' What is that Really worth?
In this celebrity Ego World. This Intuitive Knowledge;
Unequivocal suffering and the Cessation of suffering.
Remove the Suffering Remove the Untruths.
Remove the Craving Remove the Propaganda
is the Cure. Dhamma's path is the Remedy.
The Awakened One's ~ Proclamations
Buddha's Dispensation ~ 'Sasana'
Possessed of the Meaning, True Perfect Perfection.
Affected the 'MENTAL LIFE' of Humankind.
Full Moon Wisdom ~ that Discerns the Virtuous
What is good conduct? Certainly not propaganda

<u>Radiant Geometric Patterns</u>
Start imitating what, behavioral, 'Development'
Psychic Vibrations; Take Codex foods ~ they're Not holistic.
Pollution is Separation - the Whole thing's needed!
Especially as it is all Medicine for the spirit.
That's business eg. Take the Wheat market, disease has
a certain frequency. Good Radionic flakes for breakfast.
Idea of effecting inside too, smart Healthy Radar of an
Organic cereal. Start Imitating What? Propaganda Now
Resolving, the Final Puzzle. Bullshit Coke is not a Joke!!
*

<u>No Baby Doll on Bikini Atoll</u>
What landed on your beach in 1946? Not waves
of Cosmic sub ~ atomic particles but another
Little Man, Fat Boy; Uranium, Plutonium Bombs.
Why do we do this to Mother Earth?
A diabolical Experiment to destroy
the most perfect natural place.
Testing their horrors, their sick ploy
full range of nuclear radiation on her face.
What landed on your white sandy shores ~
turned it into death and concrete bunkers.
What landed in your crystal lagoons
What landed on your pristine reef ~
nothing left there now but marine grief.
Who was found responsible for this
Hellish, outrageous, terrible act?
A Crime Against Humanity
A Crime Against the Planet.
They got a medal from the Senate!
*

<u>'Dhammapada'</u>
'live in love, do your work, make an end of your sorrows'

<u>Surreal ~ Sliding Doors</u>
Resolving and Revolving.
Why do I still wake up
with the memory of her, lying beside me?
Like the feeling still of an amputated Heart.
Another poetic moment ~
another poetic moment ~
*

<u>A lustrous Vision</u>
Words keep on flowing ~
the Lotus keeps on growing
from the Mind, Loving Kind.
Waking up with a magical find.
A sense of Consciousness.
Feeling ~ for You
Beauty
*

<u>Infidel as debased as Infanticide</u>
These states are 'All Rubbish'
There's no reason even for debate.
Who accepts this, Why and How?
How far from Truth have we ourselves become.
Did they hypnotise, lobotomise you in sleep?
These acts are so ignoble, Inhumane, cruel,
brutal, heartless, pitiless, atrocious, merciless,
reprehensible, devastating, wicked, evil, unjust,
horrible, barbarous, ruthless and infinitely unkind.
Do they somehow put it in our food, inject us
with a retro virus, a manic digital frequency?
How do they capture us in this way,
that we believe they should even have a space
any sub atomic existence in our Minds?
How do they make us so Unfeeling ~

<u>Expose ½ measures</u>
Vibrational Radionics ~
All fields, auras, orbs and subtle bodies ~
biological mental astral ethereal fields.
You've created systems depleted of any energy,
no space for Clairvoyants, no room for divine
Daisies to grow and sow their healing sparkles.
Can't solve the system with modifications,
learning a bit more with painful experience.
Pollution and stress is too alien, to the Human
set up ~ needs as Poetic as a Gothic Cathedral.

<u>*</u>

<u>Diabolical Bling Bling</u>
Listen to the Cash Register sing ~
What a glorious sound the ears ring.
'On The Never Never', Ain't that Clever!
I'm sure you think so, in the Treasury
with Your Platinum 'Ipso facto'
Virtual fantasy not true Reality.
Corruption and Delusion is not fun
Credit card logos' 'Clever' repackaged Usury.
Trust in your Spirit not the dollar gun ~
Crowned with Success of even Higher debt
Abundantly blind wished you'd never met!
Same old exploitation sold as sexy glamour
hooked into it as Modern Lifestyle choices.
Don't listen to those Conditioning voices.
No more bondage as the craving slave.
Stick to the heart that's a start.

*

<u>Potential</u>
Now to tell the Best Truth.
Image of Karma effects ~
arm in arm with your child

<u>Massive Contradictions</u>
*To call Blair, Bush's poodle means you know
a lot about dogs! They're the ones Suffering it!
This is REAL! An Ultimate War Criminal.
What sort of justification can allow that?
Mrs. Quean, Mr. deaf and dumb Archbishop
in your Palaces! Lord and Lady False Morality,
Parliamentarians & other free loading parasites.
Another Crime Against Humanity, how bad is that!!*

*

<u>What is > This Inscription</u>
*In an ancient language. Dedicated to us from
Fabled Kings, Classical Sources and Sacred Texts.
How did they know! That we would lose sight
of the path ~ that we'd definitely need maps to
find the golden Treasure. & We'd need a Fix!
Our ancestors had great human compassion.
They knew from their own mistakes
of power and propaganda in the Mix.*

*

<u>The Key ~ The Soil is Magic</u>
*Millions of Unclassified micro organisms
Radioactive insects & Daisies giving Potassium,
Love Rescue Remedy ~ of their own accord.
A Natural laboratory ~ I want to smile, smile ~ can I?
Everyone wants to be Love Happy, Is there Anyone who
would not and why with any common sense would that be?
Is it the nature of the human ~ TO BE LOVE HAPPY
Instead of this continuous image from the media
our violent, ignorant, destructive, human destiny.
What would you like to nurture?
Everything under the sun the moon the stars.
Cosmic energies into life force*

<u>Frequencies ~ of It but Not In It</u>
'Born in the World, as a Lotus in the water,
growing up living in its nature ~
Now transcending ~ living untouched by it'
Those Higher level Vibrations ~
being possessed by nothing, possessing nothing
to flow freely in the boundlessness of free Spirit.
Annunciation of Love ~ truth not propaganda
Motivation to be on the Spiritual path fulfilled.
Giving from the heart ~ how about you?
Not expecting anything in return darling.
Sense of your true self not the Ego

*

<u>Observation of A Mind Set</u>
"Instead of Fighting Against Each Other, sister, brother;
We should All Be Fighting to Protect ~ Our Mother Earth"
"Patriotism is serving Pachamama all the time
and your Government sometime."
You bet Bro, another karma Drama!
Conclusions, De briefings, The Quest,
The Grail Operation ~ All Messed Up!
The Missiles went Astray over Kent.
In Very Suspicious Circumstances. Sorry.
"Pull The Other One, Heard It All Before"
I'm not A Mancunian Candidate,
from The Brain Washed Brigade.
Very Interesting Phenomenally
Worked like A Clockwork Orange.
Held 3 months Incognito, Inspection, Introspection,
in Communicado - to be Clarified then Classified.
How was that Point of View allowed to Survive?
All fucked up, Need a review of Black Ops;
by some quacking psychopath – dismissed!

Multi Phase Multiplex
Multi Lateral feelings ~
Red Rosie colours on your cheeks.
"Tell it like it is" Majesty Consciousness.
Yellow hibiscus in jasmine scented hair ~
Frangipani garlands caressing your neck,
diamonds twinkling ~
Your eyes' Surprise!
"THIS IS NOT A DREAM."
Energy Waves lapping between us,
hand in hand ~
fingers entwined,
love in the mind.
*

5th Element
Venus at the Apex
Outstretched on an Astral Pentagram
Conjoined with the messenger from Heaven
Male Female, Body Spirit, Life Death, Joy Pain,
I breathe out You breathe in
Exchange of energies
*

'It could have been the enemy'
Age of Aquarius, Christ's DNA
Zymotic Mumbo Jumbo
Zygosis and Osmosis
Breaking the Spirit
Making the Spirit
'The Walls have Ears'
The doors have fears
Bewitched cloning
garlands of gametes
A Zillion Oscillations

Activist on the Short List

What do you think of Democracy Mr. Gandhi?
"I think it would be a Good Idea"
Disrespect is based on Fear, Drummed up by?
Colonialism was so Legitimised on Ancient Civilisations.
Baghdad was once the Centre of Top Islamic Knowledge.
Not a scrapheap of blown up cars and burnt body parts.
A Babylon of Classical Texts and sumptuous hanging gardens;
Not a dump for Phosphorous shells and other Monstrosities!
This continuous cycle of Conquest being Perpetuated!
These 'Redivisions' and 'Acquisitions'
~ of the 'Spoils of War'

*

Vested Massive Miss Interests

Who's held to Account For 'Extraordinary Rendition'
Who is there to ask A Critical question without hiding?
Feel their Fear of losing their jobs & pensions, Pathetic!
The WMD. fiasco is a Perfect example. Any Reasoning?
Any legal precedence obtaining under torture, evidence?
Mind Boggling, what's become of us now, boffins & gadgets!
Resonating a very disturbed Mind with glaring Omissions.
He's not the brightest; "This is War, Nothing Personal!"

*

Delphina

You can work it out Intellectually
for revelations of liberty ~
into Mother Earth's cosmic womb
Channeling Angel voices
Exploding Stars and sonnets
A genius with the face of Krishna
combining telepathy of orgasmic true lovers
clairvoyance of her searching kisses.
Not a word Sweetheart ~ "This is Not A Dream"

Divers Ending
More than one Real World
death is merely change ~ not even
because we are Omnificent
of the Cosmic infinite scent
there are no omissions
no sins of commission
It's All Inclusive, resplendent
no end no beginning just being.
No Point but Your Divineness
Not even a diamond Omphalos.
Snowflakes fall and disappear
here a vision of eternity ~
Love is forever and together

*

'Omni' ~
Not another hotchpotch orthodoxy!
All this Stuff only causes Confusion.
Just be Sensitive to the Life force ~
that gives this magic loving energy
After My Own Heart

*

Lucus a non Lucendo
Luscious and sumptuous Metamorphoses.
She fell to Earth with a glowing Meteorite.
Voluptuous, appealing to all my senses,
"No, you haven't lost your wits!"
Lovely and glorious, a stunning sight,
exquisite, ravishing, diaphanous delight,
dazzling and gorgeously splendid
no words can describe you truly ~
Your sparkling bright eyes lit like a galaxy
radiating atomic sunbeams ~ absolutely Free

UNDERCURRENT OF LIFE STREAM

In Buddhist psychology the process of the changing mind is manifested in two levels or streams. The subconscious stream 'Bhavanga Citta' and the Conscious stream 'Vithi citta' Each one merges into the other. The subconscious stream is the hidden repository of all the impressions and memories of thoughts that pass through the conscious mind; All experiences and tendencies are stored up there, but they exert an influence over the conscious mind without it being aware of the source of this influence. These two streams of mind being conditioned by each other. The state of the active conscious mind and awareness is generally present during the day when one is awake. It is conscious of all impacts and impressions continually received from outside, through the 5 senses or of sensations received from within by way of ideas or thoughts or recollections of former thoughts. When this conscious stream which is constantly receiving sensation from within or without subsides into inactivity, as for instance during sleep, the other stream the subconscious (Bhavanga Citta) manifests ~ flowing like an undisturbed stream so long as the conscious stream does not arise to disturb it through the sense channels. When awake every time an arisen thought of the conscious mind subsides and before the next thought can arise within that infinitesimally minute fraction of time, the subconscious stream intervenes. Then when the next thought of the conscious mind level arises the subconscious stream subsides into inactivity. Since innumerable thoughts arise and fall one after another during the day, so then are there innumerable momentary interruptions to the flow of the subconscious stream during the day. The subconscious is referred to as a state of subliminal activity viz. an activity that takes place below the threshold of the conscious mind, an activity of which therefore there is no awareness on the conscious mind. The conscious stream holds only one thought or idea at a time whereas the subconscious stream holds all the impressions of all the thoughts ideas and experiences that enter and leave the conscious mind. This subconscious life stream allows us to have a memory, conditioning our thinking & action. The Bhavanga is the 'bhava'(existence) 'anga' (factor). 'Bhavanga Citta' is the indispensable factor or basis of existence. The factor of life by means of which the flow of existence or being is maintained without a break. The continuing basis or undercurrent of life, the stream of existence keeping life going. This stream of being is an indispensable condition of individual life. It is comparable to the current of a river when it flows calmly on, unhindered by any obstacle, and when that current is opposed by any thought from the world within or perturbed by tributary streams of the senses from the world without then thoughts in the conscious mind stream arise. There is a juxtaposition of momentary states of consciousness subliminal and supra ~ subliminal throughout a lifetime.

*

From '<u>Rebirth Explained</u>' by V. Gunaratna.
Buddhist Publication Society. Kandy, Sri Lanka. 1980.
This essential conscious ~ subconscious life stream is felt as a flow of sensations on the body/mind and the equanimous ~ awareness of this ever changing flow of sensations ~ 'Sampaggana Satimo' is what Vipassana meditation (as taught by S. N. Goenkaji, www.dhamma.org) uses in practice to make us realise our Inner true being ~ 'going with the flow, freedom, consciousness, transcendence, God realization beyond illusion, conditionings, ignorance, distractions, manipulations, ego trips, energetic fields, Cosmic realities, realization being now is the allowance to live in this changing Bhavanga wave of existence. See 'The Four Sublime States' Nyanaponika Maha Thera. BPS.

'Simple'
My favourite Word in India.
Being ~ happy with it ~ harmony
Meditation is everywhere ~
Divining Light
*

Journeys Out of Substitute Existences
Just Live it, You've Come Alive! Wow!
Taking Puja at the Shiva village Shrine.
You look like a very happy wreck.
let's have Wampum, no need
for bellicose threatening of War
or motiveless wanton destruction.
Once a very popular custom.
Hard to evaluate, judge it!
To see thru what it is, brother.
Early morning harmony
tapestry of our being ~
embracing with a lovely kiss
*

Peeped into transparency
Knowledge of the Supreme experience ~
what I've been led to believe....
Shown the Point of no Returns...
glimpsed a victim of Attachment.
Awesome we haven't got a clue ~ why
they would want to keep us in the dark
absorbed into infinite 'TV Programming'
never Imagined I could be beyond ~
Spiritual conquest of transcendental reality
after bathing in the waters
of Love and Compassion

Amusing Twitching Emerald Forests
Intensified human neuroses and stresses
through multi coloured Crystal lenses.
Across abstract pure white horizons
Her Father was a Shaman ~
Her Mother was a Sorceress
Her lover was a perfect connection
Amazing jet green eyes' expression.
Her child a beautiful natural creation
*
'Spirit In Sun' Sub*atomic fields of Archady are forever
Bacchus' Banquet, Dionysus' vineyards, Diana's forest glade,
Delphi's pools, springs and streams, Cupid's meadows
under Venus' starry cloak, Orpheus' Cosmic sound
impregnates Flora's shimmering, intoxicating elixir.
*
No Mind No Expectation
"The Spirit experiences the World of form and limitation in
order to evolve itself back into Conscious Union with that
Original Oneness"
*
'Osho'
"When you are utterly empty the whole existence enters you
All the stars are within you all the flowers, the Sun, the Moon"
*
'LoveLand'
I live where I feel there is the most Freedom ~
Absolutely, why wouldn't you? Freedom brings Love.
It takes Time to become Aware as a Renaissance person
to develop the insights, wisdom, the skill, the Compassion
refine understanding & let it be free as Loving Kindness
accept this highest journey, be chilled out, love yourself
~ on your way to becoming one as a Cosmic Lotus

The Blue Pill
"Guess what I got? A New dealer - doctor.
Selling Zoloff -"go to sleep, It'll be fine in the morning"
Get me out, because all the points & centre sucks!
Narrow – minded stuck to your Identity in fidelity.
Craving, Addiction, No ambition, Obsessional!
For what? My energy is focused
on being as free, Objective as I can.
Life ~ Force frequency, lose your ego,
go with whatever. 'Thank – God it's Friday"
"I'm an environmental terrorist who are You?"
"not in the package I expected, natural in her own way"
*

Vision Quests
Ethereal Cosmos ~ In tune with Earth
Participation ~ everyone shares
Could remember everything
from the furthest light year star *
into deepest dimensions of the heart.
Who has to pay for Joy?
You make your own reality, every moment
together transmutation ~ Trance free Party
comes out Whirling in the moment dancing
going back to her juices
*

Siesta
"Come Home, Pass Out"
"Spending Time with my pussy
flowing with the Babaette ~
taking wheat grass, thinking about my health.
It was horrible, still had a bit of respect left.
Love your arse, gave her a Tick Tack"
She won't know the difference ~

They Run the Matrix
'She sees it ~ Exactly for what it is'
He knows what's happening in a War! Do the boys?
"To keep a bunch of Jackasses with MI6's in Line!"
"Imposing Order in the World and Kill the People
who don't tow the Line" To be put to sleep ~
They have no Idea of Compromise; If you didn't have to.
"Fighting a War, Mad, but got balls of Male energy.
Sitting around doing nothing, nurturing a Parasite
& hatred with a Religious Zealism put on top of it.
Winding everyone up ~ Like a bunch of Toys!
Took all their Resources for Exploitation.
Outspent them on The Biggest Gun!!
Of course it's Horrible"

*

Divine Starburst
"The Illusion is Real ~ just we Identify with it" Reaction ~
Atomic galaxy central fusion. "Don't leave home without one"
The 8 directions of 'A Pedigree Party Yogi'
Sees right through it 'Soul Food' "be who I am"
That Sweet Heart ~ Who went through Hell (for you!)
Found it existing in the body & Mind. Changing Image ~
to a Good Guy, keeping the bombs out of your backyard!
Told when to Jump ~ all the strong cells survived the weak.

*

The Diamond Cutter
It's Your Mind that Operates on the Mind.
Overcome any defilements with breath
Purification of the Auxiliary Attacks.
But how to go < 'beyond' > this Mind to Space?
Deeper Awareness * Deeper Penetration
Your full trancing prayer at Shiva Valley.
Quieten ~ Calmer Concentration

Headhunting In Tehran > Shock, Awe, Horror, Terror
Ok I deserved it? "You have my head but not my faith."
'Converted many Christians by burning them with Kerosene'
"In Tolerance everybody's releasing from their Karma!"
Ok I desired them, fell on an Emperor's Peacock throne.
Reactions from the past ~ going to come back
from Saturn's Green reapers, making the Rules
in ignorance, painful vengeance until Transcendence.
"the wise don't lament for the alive or dead"
dropped Obsidian swords ~ invoking female frequency
*
Beautiful life in India
'Lucy in the Sky with Diamonds'
"No such thing as Bad drugs dude, but Bad Brain
for your Blame game. A Jackass from the beginning!"
The Smoking King ~ le Baba's magic potion....
"take LSD, sell everything and come to India" ~ Co creation,
*Procreation, Permeation, Correlation * Saraswati's darshan.*
"just because you got Democracy doesn't mean you got ~ freedom"
*
'Bonus Conspiracy'
Married a niece of Kali in Mali, painted by a Daliesque
Ingénue. "Opening more of those doors of Perception
of course they're going to put a lock on the house!"
*"Who is really living it ~ * ~ Free To Party"*
"With alcohol you don't need a lock
because You can't get out the room!"
"Breaking the taboos, biological incentives,
I'd rather have a bullet in the head."
No, I don't know about that ~ Odalisque!
Whatever Sells doesn't mean it's Good!
He's gone into the water ~

'Indices'
Diamond Crown Chakra of Mother Earth.
"Tell it like it is, Baby ~
I know deep down inside.
I believe you Love me

*

Govinda's Singing
Nothing better than the Monkey Brain
Let it run itself; Control is another opposite of Love.
You're looking at someone who's telling you
that they don't want to be with you Anymore!
"Carry your Ashram in your heart ~
You only have to Shine"

*

A Perfect Moment
It could be ~
the Rainbows
in the Sky
It's all Divine
Consciousness

*

Squatting
A bit of Freedom ~
'Not to pay the Rent' >Mortgage holiday!
We're All Rich, We're All Beautiful!
Can't be bothered about it ~ Launched it out,
let that go long time ago, on the Roller coaster.
Now I've forgotten what I was gonna say ~
Fabulous Dante, he really caught every word.
Creating Poesia, I just knew he'd been travelling
~ in India

*

'Enlightenment' ~ Smiling ~

A New Twisted drone
'US criticizes Israel for illegal use of their Cluster Bombs!'
Designed specifically to make > Their Bombs, explosives
'Explode Silently!' You can sleep Right through it!
"Hatred is the Shadow of Your Ego"
'The Opposite of Love Is Fear!'
*

*'Nectar * Contact'*
Psychiatrists don't really have a clue can you believe it?
Right off the track > Living it, Not out of a Textbook
"Couldn't even Kill a fish, that Eye's always open!"
Who has been holding the light then?
To have a House with No doors or windows.
Others swore Acid was the fuel!
The Totality of The Magic door ~
No Fear in Fearless Meditation
'Eye To Eye' not 'Eye for an Eye'
'No expectations' ~ Unexpected in a Spin!
*

Cultivation in the 'Brahma Vihara' Garden
~ the Highest Feeling towards all beings ~
*Highest Life Attaining Inner * Outer Peace together*
Pigeon holed, the Predators are out! Buddha's lesson ~
'Peace or War? ~ over a family's possession of a River.
"Is its intrinsic value more flowing with water or your blood?
No Wars were fought on behalf of dhamma, became calmer.
Peace, Impartiality & friendliness to All, after bathing
In the waters of Loving Kindness & Compassion.
Conquest > Spiritual ~ Not Political, Ego or Military
"Victory breeds hatred, the conquered sleep in sorrow.
Cast aside victory & defeat. A Peaceful one dwells at ease.
Hatred does not cease by hatred, hatred ceases by Love"
'Dhammapada'

NATUR ~ ALLY **HEART**HEART**HEART**HEART**HEART**HEART**HE ~ ART

*

My favourite woman is Venus on the terrazzo
What's the definition of 'Collaboration'?
Channeling the Art
Channeling the Mind
Channeling the Life
Channeling ~ No copyright
energy particles naturally
"I don't do dramas anymore"
because it's just a Process ~
there is no Mind, no Ego, no anything
it's just a process of changing, so be detached.
Cause and effect, action reaction is karma(if you want)
"I take care of Dhamma ~ Dhamma takes care of me" >
with those seeds of ignorance, fear, anxiety, selfishness!
Leads to not getting caught in the habit of Identifications
*Extra sensory * Galaxies & Galaxies, what to do Bubu?*
Bio Cosmic fields you call emotions, desires, ambitions,
darling, reflection of your Truest Mind in deep stillness.
I can't give the commitment you want to permanent unreality.
On a roll, no soul ~ leads to liberation
Maximum light

*

Right Time Right Place Again ~ for creative muffins
'UFO' ~ ½ ecstasy ½ mescaline, energetic fruit salads.
No Ego No Mind just a process of Inspirational change
the river changes, the body changes the Mind changes
leaving us with the BIG illusion of some unity, entity!
FREEWHEELING beyond any 'Technique' thank you
so no body, no death, no fear & terror, nothing to lose.
IT'S ONLY JUST A VERY SUPER FAST PROCESS ~

Don Quixotic vision of a marvelous Impulse
Always Keep high no abusing if using
Boggling the Mind ~
Boggling the Crown Chakra
My entry into the Universe
through your Venus Yoni ~
My entry to the nature through my Spirit
My entry to the Cosmos through my 3ʳᵈ eye.
Surprise interstellar sunrise, Mind Concept
Getting close up, keep it sweet lustful Satyr.
From the depths of Aphrodite's magical grottoes,
she is the creatrice, arriving on the plane from Moscow.
"Never use Programmed words as has been said before,
no more psychological manipulations or power games.
Let the Inspiration keep your spirit free and loving ~
dissolving moulds, realising the intentions, feeling space.
4ᵗʰ dimensional Heart calling, found what I was looking for ~
Synchronically tuned into the Ocean's morning breeze.
In your hair, in your mouth ~ every moment

*

"My Universe your Uterus, there is no mould in reality"
You put yourself on All the Spaceships ~ in Time Sense
She'll kick the door down to get free, you know how it is!
"I know who trances and I know who dances"
All of Life is a Meditation, sharing a lot of Infinity ~
Nature lets it grow, nature sending crystal snow, be clear.
Is there too much going on in your Mind, had no Idea!
Did you hear Krishna singing? Such beautiful melodies..
With the US cavalry out on Location, where are they now?
Camp Euphrates with gruesome bloody red Taliban talismen.
Drop the Image ~ "My Heart Is Broken"
'Reflecting it back onto Itself'

Neurological (Emotional physical psychic) disorders et al
These disorders put into the context of a 'Zero Tolerance'
An Usurper or A Despot Characteristic - for those with the
Power to destroy a culture, putting us all to nuclear swords!
*Effecting all Species All our DNA strands * forever, from our*
neighbours, partners, child, teacher, pope, President, Mother,
Father, your favorite celebrity or influencing a Star from afar!
This World is paying the Price. Mother Nature is paying with
our Invisible fears, traumas, greed, nightmares, 'disorders'
How would most of us ever know or be able to comprehend
the effects on our beings, nerves, emotions, actions, feelings?
Don't ask anyone with ADHD to be the Emperor. Did anyone
Analyse that preserved Brain of Lenin or Mind of Mr. Mao?
Did we ever Psychoanalyze the decisions of Hitler, Nixon, or
any other 'Hero's DNA'; Napoleon a well adjusted General!
What about Genghis Khan a fine Empire builder or Caesar1,
another amazing bringer of Civilisation to Barbarians living
peacefully on undiscovered pagan coasts; What is this Mind?
Buddha had an answer Jesus & Krishna gave excellent advice
to the rains of terror falling and cluster bombs dropping from
the sky on your family. Making hereditary codes which we still
live with in our deep sub consciousness, it's still Manipulating!
Thought I saw a Dinosaur eating my wife "don't freak out mate"
Lie on your back & look into the clear night sky to get a sense
of how You are the way You are; Why & Who; ~ What to do?
We are born into this we even bring it with us for R/evolution
There is this undercurrent Magma effecting us all, take a look
at its potential 'disorders' their countless links & subsections
bubbling up Consciously /Unconsciously in us and in those of
beings around us, affecting us, destroying us, loving you & me.
Allowance of this reality, 10% we think we know, what about
90% the rest? 'What The Bleep' & what about Transcendence
of this Omniscient Mind, realising our true Omnipotence ~

"The Plant is telling you"
White Lines ~ You call Right Wrong and Wrong Right.
Total Perversion ~ A lie is a lie is a lie is lying ~
"Consumed by Obsession, greed not freed to handle it."
Not consumed by Addiction, It can handle it, can you?
She has the Brain of Brains, Spiritual Sexuality
keeping energy ever going higher up the psychic hot wire.
Kingdom of Heaven is the Ultimate ~ where Children are free.
Paradox, concept of Perfection; It's Perfect, no Stress.
"Re/Scramble the Mind, don't use Conditioning words"
"I have Peace Man, I can't describe it, I am Content"
I'm growing, Plants getting the light; No day or night.
Clean Crystal giving Perfect sight; Vibrate ~
"How can I give you more when your cup is full?"
*Constant flowing cosmic energy * fulfilling Oceans' infinity*
*

Kailash Air
"Just following the path all the way to China.
You need a special guide" Cold hungry nights.
Legends & roots of Paradise on Earth. 'Shangri-La'
Market of a ruined city with frankincense and Myrrh.
She passed the Shrine of Vishnu the Preserver
If you answer with a True heart ~
took him to the Crystal Mountain
there they first made love in a sacred landscape.
Shiva & Parfait Parvati's honeymoon, ethereal dawn.
Lake Manasovra, Centre of this Planet of the Mind.
Different conceptions of Time & Space ~
Hidden in stupendous valleys at the End of this World.
Met the serene Consciousness of a Grand Magician.
She'd joined a caravan of Yak herders to Shambala.
Following Prophecies of Padma found in ancient sutras.
Led an expedition to find the source of Ma Ganga

Surreal Ocean
Kind for kind, on the lake of your Mind
More than the dance to the Supreme ~
If you crash your car you get a new one.
Got a different one here. You had it (death)not rebirth
'Atman' just words, it is there, 'Soul' is just there.
*The Mind blowing * bubbles ~ isn't it…*
Just to survive here you have to be Spiritual!
Prophets everywhere, gorgeous 'No Woman No Cry'
Reality mish mash, jolly, shanti Boddhisattvaette
on the way to a jungle beach, under a Banyan tree.
Flew in on a spiral of love, kept her in reach
cooing as a dove, Spirit of Cupid in the air.
Vedic mathematics, deatomiser, dematerialized
passed the door, walked through the walls ~
dropping out using 5 elements & Vishnu's wife.
Build a church, Open a business for sinners.
Vedanta ~ men free of desires, but tempted!
Unnatural, only Shiva can give rebirth ~
Formlessness can take any form that's given to us.
Lakshmi's blessing ~ Abundance has everything.
*
*

*River with the Colorado Corazon of Sur*reality*
Love show live show off the hook, sorry I drifted off ~
*full of hot desire, full power * black nights sparkling*
in emerald crusted eyes she flies without disillusionment.
Timeless multi dimensionality on an Amazonian dusty road
Finding natural peoples finding natural harmony ~ sailing
a boat up Rio Branco searching for female diamond shoots.
*Opening up her petals like a bee * impregnating orchidees.*
Gently inside, full Shamanic inspiration to wet tantric roots.
Feeling divinely ~ to discover sublimely her rapture in mine.
*It's bright at the beach of Supra * Orgasmic Consciousness*

Astral 'Padmophul' Petals

Perceptual ~ perpetual floating in a light golden lily pond.
Finite body/mind: Immersion into Infinite formlessness
Saw you in a dream>*< met you in a long lovely poem.
Enlightenment Transcendence Liberation
of the memory, Ego, form, conditioned identity, Patterns>
Free of Your Mind, limits, Pain, into limitless Cosmic reign
Formlessness & its 'Omkar' beingness ~ silence all around
Free of concepts of a Planet; 'Reality' of 'Mother Earth'
'Nature' as the ever ~ changing everlasting Universal energy.
Stream of Consciousness ~ being * growing in natural Daisy.
Don't get caught up in the 'Material' delusion, Illusion of it.
Somehow being the most Real ~ Realise the boundless Forest.
Now how to do that? In the midst of Maelstroms in the trees ~
gusting Tantric thrusts of your desire * Just to be ~ to be frees
Expression of it in my art; Feelin' it in my sub * atomic heart ~
Let the body go > as rocket boosters falling away in free flight
Even with dyspraxia, yes amazing to have this Full realisation.
"Senility wasted on most people" put into 'Cosmic Conscious'
Lost the Yangste Dolphin today 'Extinct' gone forever, where?
No more Karma ~ Became part of the Universal Ocean ~ now
Fighting with your mother's cancer, its existence, frequency ~
Realise your own true 'beingness' & her Infinite Spiritualness
let the big Attachments go ~ knowing we're all Radiant flow ~
There are innumerable disorders on this Earth to suffer or not
naturally & those Conditioned; Ignorance, Karma, Identities!
People around us are living with these, knowing & unknowing
Affecting each of us in our 'Environment' ~ our Relationships.
We can't Control it all! It's happening ~ Being Conscious of it,
empathise, put it into perspective. Whatever happens we are all
part of a greater boundless Cosmic consciousness. Accept that
Let it go, know the body is not your deeper essence, being ~ flow
ALL IN ONE ~

<u>Faithfully</u> ~ Fell from Pagan Pleiadies
"It's a lot for a liver to take"~ Atom Bomb on Fire
or Marilyn Monroe cavorting with a Coke bottle!
Pulsing balls of Light. Battleships in a Sky of hungry Comets.
Goa gives me something to dream about! 'Definitely * maybe'
Chillin' out at Scarlet's, I must be the luckiest guy in the world.

*

<u>Peas</u>
Going through
A Process ~ Processed
Processing
& fresh fig juice ~
Poetical not geometrical.
Not Violating fundamental principles
of rare green Iridescent spiders

*

<u>Sunkissed Spirulina</u>
Full Orbs of light * Golden white rays, Haloe Veras juices ~
Making love with a resentful, disdainful, haughty ladybird.
Do you know what you've done with my soul, baby!?
Where's the sense in that, Blasting from the past.
Pile your way thru it, no messing, dumped, denied.
Straight through the pain ~ if you've accepted that one.
Straight through guilty barricades

*

<u>Red Blue and Pirate White</u>
Rewriting the Rules, of Engagement Book.
Lied to the Whole World on Prime Time TV.
Can't sell it ~ Another Massacre to the Public.
'<u>Liberating</u>' >>Your Gold! Give me a break!
It's All about <u>Plunder</u> (& 'Stressing Techniques!')
Hand in Hand; They Vote with a Shotgun in Dixie.
Mr. Bush campaigns in rattlesnake Cowboy boots

Buddha shares his loving Kindness
Seeing you in wonder off the battlefield
All perfected ~ body is Immaterial, infinity.
Sitting, feeling hot Kundalini rising in your Yoni
Individual Star crossed lovers of eternal entity ~
(BG.ch2.39) Yoga free from bondage, being bliss.
Living without the fruit of a throbbing Karmic tree.
'Samadhi', from the Vedic dictionary; 'Fixed Mind'
When the Mind is fixed for Understanding the Self.
Not possible for those captivated by the senses ~
condemned by the processes, of Material Energies.
Be 0 free from all dualities, from any gainful anxieties;
Be established in the self (yoga). Have no guilt feelings!
Pain & fear because you're Attached to the Sensations!
Lovely to read the poetry of Vyasadeva & dance at dusk
on a Starlit beach
*

Lila Pastime
'Her disorders are only sense perceptions'
Met her in a State of cosmic trance
*in a dance * full on hot Romance*
"don't grieve for the destructible body by knowing
inconceivable immutable Invisible all pervading
eternal energy ~
Always existing, undying, primeval
free by witnessing, not forgetfulness
swimming in streams of consciousness.
She is spread all over you ~
changing in front of your eyes & Inside of you.
We'll change and meet in another body.
I'll kiss pure spirit on your wet lips ~
In another destiny we'll mix our energy.
Eternally you & me ~ forever free

<u>In the heart of every atom...</u>
Beyond Man's reasoning powers, understanding ~
Absolute Truth; Teaching the philosophy of devotion.
Plants growing flowers under the Lotus feet of Krishna
fully absorbed ~ as a fish lives in water.
Engaged in Transcendental loving, even poorest of poor ~
Offering their genuine love ~ simplicity, a leaf of a flower.
*

<u>Heron Spirit ~ Not for a Program</u>
"Colours for measuring Space"
Atmospheric Painting ~
'Olive & Mustard'
'Yellow & Rose' ~ 'Orange, lemon & Violet'
'Reds with Green Emerald discs, in a synchronised field'
with Imaginary, Incandescent Skies and Vertical light.
Stripes and bands of Visual language * Unique Images
Sensations for your Sensuous Awareness to make 'Real'
'Tradition, patterns, textures, colour, size, tone, line.
Created Cubist grammar, Illusions of perspective, reflective,
bending planes of colour, rendering forms in deep space.
How not to lose the abstractness of an Image'
~ simply by going out of an open window.
Liberation of a Sub ~ Conscious light frequency.
*

<u>The Earth Is A Living Being</u>
Death through Pleasure ~
Losing the Highest Treasure?
A Man Made biological Weapon.
Cold hearted person, a 5* Reptile.
For you, Invasion nothing to do with bad Karma.
You're a destroyer or a Weapon of the destroyer!
Big Time Invasion Plans, Heavy Metal in Nagarland
Material Mind's gone Haywire! Once tribals were free...

Discernment
The Experience
Is there to allow ~
to Realise the differences
through our Judgments.
Learning in the duality
growing in the moment
Pressed into a diamond
to shining Crystal
Human being
*

Fundamentalist hormones
You Can't always be spiritual or compassionate or be
able to care for your old parents or dedicate your self.
Have to give yourself space & time and know your ego.
Making a vow (consciously?) to love & honour another
person in sickness & in health until death us do part"
Don't make your self a guilty prisoner in a box or her!
Can't always Identify in Buddha or Krishna's doctrine
need a sense of freedom to break the Iron chains of Will.
Determination of a Zealot to take it All too seriously dear!
"I am Sujata, please take a break & have refreshment Sir"
*

Venus Cream
Chasing Diana to a forest glade.
Chasing a dragon into the stream
Sky pilot with Psy*chicks in hot pursuit.
"And I was blissed & blessed"
One drop went on a sugar lump ~
Saw me going out of my body ~ later
Astral projections inside your brain.
I managed to get my shoes off & my head went 'Twang!'
"Don't fight it Feel it"

Dreaming into the Present
To keep on being creative follow your passion ~ finally.
Instead of having a golden chain around your neck
of course and effect, the process of living.
No one there; Only an ego there if you manifest one.
Arising remaining passing away, growing breathing.
Atomic energy with a Mind that shines out to the stars.
No one there, never was never will be, identity of illusion.
Beginningless beingness streams of consciousness ~
"life is a deep sleep of which love is the dream"
*

'Blacking out'~'un trou de memoire'
'break up in time or die in time. You have to let go ~ that's ok'
You'd definitely go down with that ship. Deep in the heart
in her Temple of Heaven * looking down over Venus
*

'Saumya ~ Vapuh' Sansk: The Most Beautiful Form
Surrender Your Self, Your Mind, Your thinking Ego ~
Use your Mind and body to do this especially when down.
When the ego is weak, at the rock bottom, in a mess, zero,
lost with no hope ~ Surrendering becoming Humble, once
in your life. Use this Experience to let Mind 'disorder' ~ go.
This is a Uniquely special moment although you're too busy
Suffering to see it, to go beyond the Pain. It doesn't have to
be a Complete tragedy. This is the silver lining, it takes you
through the Gates ~ Like Arjuna not wanting to fight a War;
'Those who are wise lament neither for the living nor the dead,
Know the Unknowable; Absolute Truth of a Surrendered Soul'
See Krishna through Spiritual, non material eyes of Revelation.
*

'Night Watch' ~ A Russian Horror Film!
"Are the Ingredients Important or The Effect?"
"The World hasn't changed, just You"

70

Spirituality
Materially free
*of Time * Space*
Transcendentally
*

Ad. Fist
Passively aware ~ Sitting by a river
Challenging my Mind ~ Creating Inspiration.
"Dreams Are Good ~ Their Reality Is Even Better"
*

Suicidal Fish
'Sleep walking through life' or awake while dreaming
Wired differently in your brain, psychomotor epilepsy
It was an 'Accident' no such thing as 'Zero Tolerance'
Heissenberg's Principle, Can't be 100% sure of anything.
Transported Mentally, changes in Self Awareness ~
Normal functioning, complex behaviours, automatisms;
Organic brain syndrome what is the Chemical Catalyst?
Footprints in Time Waves
*

Hoping for a speed dating Geisha from Eurasia
Pimpness the male sponsor, keeping them in line
like sleepy Caterpillars, hooking up the hookers.
'Cut to the Quick' "You make me fuckin' sick dear!"
Trippy dimensions, 'Girls with Kickstands Welcome'
get rid of all those parameters; Politics bad everywhere.
Joy passing the debacle; A body buzzing like a drill.
Krishna laughing
*

'Polaris' ~ The Ultimate Doomsday Fish
swam into Scottish waters, 'Holy Lock!'
Targeted on Glasgow (3rd largest city).
Nuclear Armament ~ spells Disaster!

71

<u>*Where did you learn your 'Detention Techniques?'*</u>
Forbidden to have mosquito nets in the red mosque.
We can't hear the monks chanting only screaming!
They shot him 7 times in the head, 'A Hard Stop'
Used '124 grain' ammunition. Dead to Brain > before
the body could react, to hold up his hand & say "Why?"
What about the 'State Peace and Development Council'
A Genocidal junta in the land of dhamma, like so many!
And the World, UNO. Sit on their hands again; Useless!
Models of War ~ Guantanamo Bay to Abu Ghraib Prison.
International Laws all flew out the window; When they
let General Pinochet walk out of the court a free man!
When Demons are left excused, corruption lives in us.

*

<u>*"My home is Tuscany"*</u>
Dreamy house amidst rolling hills & countryside.
An Assignation in beautiful atmospheric Firenza.
Nymphs discovered dancing on Etruscan Carvings
lying in village pools outside Sienna.
Swans wildly animated by her scent.
"Leave all your troubles behind"
Keep that breath for Planting trees, they won't listen to me.
We are here for a reason; Thought I ~ was Mad.
Keeping the balance, stepping into Beautiful Umbria.
A bridge crossing to a Portal of energies.

*

<u>*Kama Sutra Yoga*</u>
69 asanas with an Indian Tantra Goddess Rati.
Multi fingered, six armed dancing Shiva in heat.
They're not his creations, they're finite Self creations.
Children don't quench his thirst for spirits of the World.
"Your life is the creation of your Mind" Now Looking out
to the Stars ~ Polishing his lingham in the naked sun ~

The Model
I have Nothing to cause problems with other egos ~
Already living creatively, inspiration and love freely
Wonderful chilling out at the psychedelic German Bakery.
Being part of an ecological sustainable community,
to get to the beach navigate around 15 coconut trees
while a Diva plays the heavenly flute to 'Om Shanti'
Big green gathering of my laughing friends.
Keeping the Mantra consciously in the heart
A Buddha field beside the Arabian sea.
*

Intuition
More Meditation
~ on nothing
*

She came on the still wind
She appeared from Solar radiation
Stars in your eyes Astral traveller
Who wrote those lines?
Their intention took you to paradise.
They stayed for the monsoon always smiling.
Frequencies of Tantra love,
overlooking the river
Ecstasy ~ at dawn waking together on the balcony.
Making Puja to his lingham, giving fruit to her Yoni.
Screaming in the Jungle at night
*

Alternatives
Have you ever heard of 'Spiritual Democracy'?
Land by the Sea ~
Astral space in your face
A child in your smile
'Namaste'

'No One Dies ~ Just A Process of Dying in a Cosmic Ocean'
'The Earth Is A Living Being'~ multi dimensional energy.
It's manna food ~ on the Level of Inspiration.
Learning how to speak, to Communicate, to feel, to peak.
"I'm Not trying to paint, I'm expressing being with the flow"
She really don't have a clue what she put us through!
'Absolutely Bananas' name for my shop, "Come See"
'To Obey or Not to Obey; To Pay or Not to Pay'
That is the question, if you still really need one!
You're as Free as you want ~ to be, supposedly.
I'm a Sun Worshipper going for bright vital light.
To the Master a lie is the beginning of darkness.
Listening to the whiles of Satan, a seductive Voice.
"Eve come here" ~ making every thought captive!
*

'Syndrome'
"Everybody's different
but we expect everybody
to be the same"
My lover was afraid of being touched!
Hot ~ It's all Maya
I feel like an Angel at the end ~
The life is to change, be here now
"The end of something is always
the beginning of something new"
dancing of Nataraj
*

'Life is only a story
If you believe it or not'
Having too much Fun #1
In the Vastness of the Land.
'Propaganda of War'
"I try to Love Everyone & so loving myself"

74

"Love * gives you Energy ~ It moves"
He got away in a Psychedelic Rainbow car ~
be yourself, be who you are, be who you want.
Death ~ 'believe in the Miracle frequencies'
"the end coming ~ from Sense Perception"
It's no body's fault *LIVING * MEDITATION.
Life is Alive ~ It belongs to the Universe.
It's All one, go wherever you want to go ~

*

Just a Movie Screaming
You want a drama, a thriller, Romantic comedy, tragedy!?
A Rainbow, an act of God, not light refracted thru a Prism!
Pure Existence Is In You
Not just what your amazing Brain Manifests. And which ~
Hemisphere is being Operated for You & Your achievement?
Right or the left ~ being Creative or Controlled > Organised.
10% capacity use? What is your Intention? Acting in that vein ~
You're a pain ~ in the balls; I took my tent to where eagles are.
Luminous & Shape shifting ~ bouncing back or cracking up?
"America Please Don't Come Here and Help these People"
flying cups and saucers

*

Toxic Tom, he knows the Planet.
Will you dance with Charley Chang -
Will you dance with six armed Nataraj or Mr. Metal?
Let the Universe Roll ~ Let Maya play out her role.
On a Higher Level ~ You have many many hearts.
Came from Venus Energy * knocking at Your front door!
Creating your Own Matrix! Manifesting the challenge.
Always come back to the center, passing out of the storm.
Coming from a clear Open heart.
"Please ~ give me a ticket to the nearest place by the sea!"
Took her kids to the Refuge center in Cornwall

Revolution at the barricades
"The purpose of Mindfulness and the four sublime states was
to neutralise the power of the ego that limits human potential.
Instead of saying "I Want" the Yogin would learn to seek the
good of others; Instead of succumbing to the hatred that is the
result of our Self ~ Centred greed; Use compassion and good
will. When these positive, skillful states are Cultivated with
Yogic intensity, they can root themselves more easily in
Unconscious impulses of our Minds so becoming habitual.
Four Sublime states are used to pull down the barricades
we erect between ourselves and others in order to protect
~ the fragile ego" ('Buddha' ~ Karen Armstrong)
*

Bhakti Baba.
Living Life Free
Free free free free free free free free free free
Watering the seed, growing the flower.
Cosmos of Stars in blossom
Filled with desire
deep Inside you
blissful fire
*

Kali ~ Maya can drive anyone mad
I got a Text from England.
Daffodils * blooming ~
Blackbirds are laying eggs.
Longer days and Golden Sunsets
Find the 'Space'
Allowing the form to be
You are the action ~
Free whirling helping them go on the journey.
Everything is Simple ~ natural
as a Rock ~ Is God

'Republic' ~ Swept it under the Carpet!
Full of Bananas all over India (& the rest!)
Lots of Bananas in the mythical Indian ~ Democracy
there's as many Bananas as on Carmen Miranda's head.
In the Indian Justice System, lots of expensive, Ripe Bananas.
Most people living in Indian Villages swallow dal & Bananas
Traditionally growing nothing but Bananas, eating Bananas.
And what do they have in common with Honduras? Bananas!
You can get away with Rape & Murder, killing with Bananas?

*

'Indian Science Fiction'
Sita beside the Lankan Ocean.
Alone battling light & darkness.
Here to provide a Conscious alternative.
A balance ~ to all the shit in the World!
I can survive in India, the Goa tribe,
the rest of the country a Spiritual vibe ~
We can do everything between us ~ meeting
the most amazing people just sitting there
passing the time of day together with a smile.
*'On a divine mission' * lights of a Cosmic Rishi*
walking from Kanya Kumari, Orissa, to Gangotri.
Children of Auroville to a Yogi Painting at Cholamandel.
"Hari Rama, Hari Krishna" playing Psy trance to lovely Radha

*

Party
We called him lucky Pierre.
Wanted to score, took a Pill.
Invitation to a Psyber Solstice.
"Follow the Police helicopter"
Looking for Aussie dread lockers
Giving out Roses ~
Ready to perceive & receive them

How to switch off the attachment?

Spiritual Alchemy

"When You're happy you got wings on your back ~
Reposez vos oreilles a Goa; We're only one kiss away"
'It's the Universe' We are the Moon, we are the Arctic seabed,
we are Green land too brother, You are the hurricane
on the streets of Houston, we are COSMIC.
Don't let anyone tell you that
"You are not from the Quantum Crystal Space Ship."
"You are a little Planet" 'A jewel in the Sky'
"Welcome Aboard" ~ "Welcome to Earth"

*

Ayuhuasca ~ On the Rainbow diet
'Loanwalla' 'getting loans made easy' & sexy!
Poverty can wipe out your morals real quick.
Sitting on the street drinking a Mai Tai ~
watching people being mugged, by the Police!
The Economy is collapsing, water wars, freaky greedy patterns
Living in a cardboard box, lucky, too many people are homeless!
Where is the balance, is there a balance for our Mother Earth?
Choosing cheap ethanol for your car or feeding starving Darfur?
People drinking Biofuels without any Ice! What are we doing?
Everything goes up with the price of bread ~ Consequences!
The Rivers will dry up! Where is the natural realisation?
I wouldn't hold your breath.
"the Sun is getting hotter darling"
Is this all bullshit just to get new higher Carbon Taxes?
"We know the sea is coming"

Happy
'Enlightenment' can wait ~

*

Lao Tsu Creativity
"The more you know
the less you understand"
"It's the now ~ It's always been about the now
And it's Wild!

*

Observing
Discipline that Mind
Meditation is Silence.
Easier to skin up
Beauty of the herb.
"Seen people panicking going to a Yoga class!"
Promises me Peace.
Controlling the Mind, seeing 'the path'
Don't want to live by Expectations, Rules but...

*

AC. Gravitation
"The Earth only exists
for Sense gratification."
Awareness ~ enjoying all Its distractions.
Sex the same High - refractions
All to do with Vibration ~
The Maya Planet.
Rising in flames to the Heavens
When you were formed.
*That Magic touching, her 3rd eye * Clear no Mind.*
Golden bindoo rays of a Dhamma beauty Queen.
Put her under 'House Arrest' for being an Avatar.
Meditating in silence ~ for Peaceful Revolution.
Miracle after Miracle after Miracle ~ changing

Yeah Lotus Eater
Interface with the Best, the Top.
What do you do with it? Go Mad with it
Enjoy It ~ It's beautiful and very Precious
What to do? Love it

*

A Coke head
'He Spanked the High Life'
"I'm hanging out with a load of Crazies!"
Let the river lead you to the Ocean ~

*

A Sacred Pyramid
Billy Graham Where's the Spirit ~
Exploding into another dimension!?
Showed me the book 'Practical Demon Keeping'
Are they on a New vine?
Mystical foundation can't put it into words.
"I went AWOL, took me off my ship
Sent me to Live on a submarine in Hawaii!"
Who would really want to hurt anyone?
A common slave, give me 1.5 lakh
And I'll put him on the local Police Force!
Release it, Stop the Mind's ~ Unconscious movements.
You have to tell > The Mind to 'Shut the fuck Up'
Expand your Pure Mind ~ listening to Music.
Judgmental, duality, which is death, good or evil?
'Tree of Knowledge'
Observer & Experiencing ~ being in the Allowance.
'Tree of Life'
Not in parameters ~ freestyle, no separation.
"Yoga is discipline, Tantra is Integration"
Magic with Children ~ Enormous Fun.
Everywhere the present is the presence

Breaking out of a Shell
The World Empire serving Satan Babble.
Lord God Nimrod cruising the Milky way
After the flood ~ Separated them with different tongues.
The key to Acid ~ Be Open. Embrace ~ the Universe

*

'Get A Grip!'
"Ain't no Love like your Love"
throbbing drum on her hip, cheeks lip to lip
Person to Person ~ Face to Face

*

Sufi
'Rumi left Religion
for a relationship
with * Divine'
Walking with light

*

'The Enfields just started turning up'
The Light streaming through your eyes darling
Timeshare "You've won a Ukrainian dream bride"
Believing in the Temptation and the Winning
A corrupt Casting Agent; what do you expect?
And They say Krishna said it was True ~
Channeling beyond the money energy.
There's not the answer, looking in the wrong place.
You've won the lottery in India, "It was Me!"
Your number's come up!

*

Fluffy Hallucinations
"It's more with being in tune"
Crystal clear
Hyperchondriacs.com in the first place.
The thing is Not to get in this shit!

Tao Mountain
"Everything will be good!"
"I was just Shining"

*

Natural beauty of Love
Watching the Mud (mind) hole bubbling.
"I understand E motion, I am Emotional!"
Mind has been Conditioned for 100000000's of years!
Want to go back to the Natural State, "Welcome to earth"
Wise man Purring with a green eyed Persian pussy on his lap
"let go of it"
Switch*/To Feeling.
Stay Inside your body
Universal Rhythm
Align Your Brain with it ~ the Cosmic energy.
"You Are The Stars" Nevertheless still True.
Who can complain ~ when it's sunny every day?
It's the mother who makes life ~ things come to be.
We Worship the Spirit, female elementals.
Cosmic dancing all about Creation being

*

Perfect Finish
We don't have to sell ~ ourselves any more.
You Are The Gift
Already

*

All in The Cerebellum
Mantras from your Mind
"In Spirit there is No caste"
Free from Mind body heart.
What's left? Just You

Frequencies of the Sun
The Living Proof, 'A Living Legend'
We're all Babes in the eyes of the Universe.
Partying since the Stone age.
The Bad old days, burning Eve at the Stake;
Chopped off another Consort's noggin.
No goin' back, it's all within.
'Noblesse Oblige'~
'Privilege entails Responsibility' oh yeah!
An Ethiopian on the Ether Net setting up deals for a 'Coffle'~
Train of beasts, slaves fastened together. Oh yeah, too true!
Everyone can be who s/he wants ~ Accepting Happiness.
Not Guilty for feelings of having Fun, fancy free.
Detached self, so no problem no victim, easy ~
Lights up like a big glowworm in heat.
Losing your rights, what do you know?
Leave it to the Universe ~
Chimps in trees with tomahawks; Now I know the ropes!
*How to see with your Heart * more & more feeling*
*Open * Portal for the docking Soul*
To Receive ~ All Information
*
*

With the moment
Realisation In the Rainbow
Making a biochemical Mandala
Sacred Geometry
Mudras opening up the circuits
In your electromagnetic field.
'Psychiatrists have highest rates of suicide
They become 'Mental' Off their rockers.
Attached themselves to problems.
Then there's the Dentists dead in the surgery.
And Italians burning candles for your soul

No Separation
'You're in Love or You're Not in Love'
Lovely
*

St. Germain's Synergy
'Who wants to go to the Dubai Shopping Festival?'
And Who wants to go to the Next Level?
When you are in Tune everything comes ~
Singing Tones having the right frequency
found the harmony in a vibrating throat chakra.
Connection to the Emotion, Realises the Idea * in the Heart.
What was the Intent? How to be a Cosmic Samaritan.
Singing human mantras in this dynamic Global World.
Don't be cynical, building Resonating Toning Pyramids
Already given to us ~ flying all the time in there
*

Puja Bhakti
"She took her shoes off at the door"
Made a good pipe of Opium ~
You don't get aggressive,
smoking on Public buses.
"Give them what they want to see"
*

A Field of Peaceful Protons
The Love that fills you up
The Real you ~ Recognising Yourself in everything else
In the Vibrating Temple of your heart
Looks like everywhere else but here!
The future coming as the Present flow ~
Tactics of the Mind to escape the beingness ~
Needs a Sense of Time to manifest in the space
You can truly only make a 'Plan' ~ for Now
'Enjoy This Moment It Never Stops' ~

<u>Discovered the Q field on Monday night</u>
Positive effects of natural energy from the primeval forest ~
on people's behavior and moods who are feelin' they love it.
'80% of jungle destruction within 30 Kms. of every main road.
1/5 cut down, used for cattle ranching, in the hands of the few!'
Effects of Observers, on exploiters in the Amazon quantum field.
When you look particles snap into position, jungle's destroyed!
Experiencing many possibilities at once ~ collapsing on the One
Multiple probabilities your sub conscious into Amazon's species
Doing your best to fine tune the field, not obliterating the trees!
<u>*'Space is just the Illusion that everything is Separated ~ dualities'*</u>
Everything is still touching ~ entanglement in a Spiral Universe
Seen by a naked eye dancing with Gaia across a milky way sky.
Twirling through Multi dimensions together at exact same time

*

<u>'Stereoscopic Magic In front of your Eyes'</u>
'Indivisible * Inseparable ~ in 3000 positions instantaneously
Giving the Mind an Intention to dream, cleansing a Sacred site.
Imprint ~ conditioning the space to a higher level of Symmetry.
Are people's thoughts affecting the World/Reality we see? Oui.
'Emoto' ~ Projecting love and thankfulness to water elements
Blessed beautiful Zen crystals, Chi of love ~ 90% in your body
Driving force of your Consciousness, your nature, your heart.
What can our own thoughts do to Ourselves, darling?

*

<u>Moving back down the time line</u>
How do you see the world, city, ghetto, tribe, nuclear frequency
Focusing coming back to us mentality attuning to what is what?
6 >10 seconds and we lose the Attention Span, destiny of Man!
Deepest Consciousness creates Universes, finds spiral galaxies
Mind as superficial or Profound energy density ~ ShivaShakti
Only Spending time; It's our own Addictive needs defining us!
Reflected not affected, "I Love You" Chi what thought can do!

<u>Challenging Dogma of the law</u>
'Dualism of the Seen and Unseen'
"Unlocking mysteries of time ~ space geometry
Connections to the Universe ~
Needs a New Quantum * Vision, perception
What Makes It Work For You?
New Spirituality * Atomically * has an Impact
How does your Memory, Mind, Heart react?
We're All Connected ~ as Live human beings.
Consciousness is Real, not untrue Propaganda;
Separation, Alienation, Isolation, Mistaken view!
Brain Processing, Fine tuning ~ Experiences of
Our Senses. 'We don't Know what Reality Is!'
Filtering 400 million bits of Info. each second
(thru our sentient fields) (only aware of 2000)
(Brain's receiving it, we haven't integrated it)
"If it's Real I Want To See It ~ to Feel it"
Being the Editor of Sensory Information.
Delusional Paranoia <> Assigning ~
Rational Probabilities > of what my eye sees
of what my eyes tell me ~ it's gorgeous!
Hallo sin nation *^* What is deceiving us?
What Is The Real Reality?
New neural grids of realization.
CONTEMPLATION

*

<u>Ironic Elementals of a Mandarin</u>
"You can't cheat the Universe" ~ Turning reality on its head,
upside down. Seeing Consciousness as a threat or as a clown!
Said, Jesus Christ was a heretic; Status: holy subversive Alien
& the Dalai Lama, Super Mr. Big, Tibetan fanatical Terrorist!
Aung San Suu Kyi, dangerous ninja to a dhamma life country!
Seeing Consciousness in a Heart ~ not coercive rattling sabres

Forbidden Zone Surprise

Sails down the Nile touching Isis' swinging Platinum Pendulum
Coming Inside the Crystal sacred pools of resplendent Osiris.
Balancing a feather, Sacred Geometry in Horus' astral eyes.
Cosmic sound of silence dances in your beating heart & veins.
People's behavior is always amazing, try living with a hermit.
Her house above an olive grove ~ along the Aegean sea shore
playing on the steps surrounding azure Temples of Poseidon.
Sea green eyed sultry Nereids & dreams not going to happen.
She sailed alone for the Isle of Boi Pepa, you'll bring her back.
A young nymph growing into a vibrant Goddess, Radiantly ~
Introduced me to buried desires, flames of Vestal Priestesses.
To see the most beautiful body, shimmering skin, in this world.
Holding herself over me ~ feeding all her loving needs.
Sprinkling Golden showers on our starry seeds.
This Ocean is Real ~
Her screams of ecstasy are Real, really loud!
*

The Violet Upanishad

Jupiter's daughter wading naked from marine foam ~ Wow!
The cryogenic 'Venus Anadyomene rising with the sultry heat.
Revolutionary higher energies, solving all the hidden mysteries
*How are all the forces of the Universe Interacting * Vesta?*
Acting reacting on matter; Do you have an answer to anything?
Look into my eyes, protecting Ceres not your amulets of sorcery.
Holding the force that acts on every star in the Universe.
Gravity all around us
*

Edgar Cayce's Stasis.

"All healing comes from the divine within. Hate, malice, and
jealousy only create poisons within the mind, soul and body.
To be sure attitudes do influence the physical conditions of the
body, no on can hate his neighbour and not have liver trouble"

The Black Paintings
New Age ~ of doubt and disenchantment.
War>'the Carnival of death'
"Join us for the longest Siesta in history"
Yes 'Organically grown ~ Not built'
New Spirits of Inclusiveness ~
Art of the future not of the Failure.
Barking wild dogs, at the end of the song ~
Nothing but fear walking in a trembling Paseo.
Carpeted Guernica with bombs of horrific Suffering!
"Accept our differences and Use them"
Learning the language of dreams.
*

Repatriated In Transcendence
With Full Military Honours.
Draped in a National Flag. "that's OK then ~"
You have to be really Cosmic ~ to accept gratefully that one!
Everything's OK. let it be & reflect from it ~ Learn from it.
Allow the Madness with no attachment.
Accepting it as part of changing 'Reality'
It is now ~ Show us how to respond.
*
-
'Money Is No Object'
What we see is in the eye of the Mind.
If I'm quiet she'll be none the wiser.
They Blasted them to Kingdom come!
'Free' ~ Markets, free to be as greedy as they want!
Free to be honest, you have a beautiful face.
Liquidator takes the loot and looks the other way.
It crossed my Mind; The 'Emperor King' equation.
'Meditation helps us realize these cherished false beliefs'
'If there was a place where one didn't exploit other beings!'
& are not Insulting to Cosmic life force…

Their Vulcan Branch
Al-Qaida is CIA.- they do what they're told & when to do it.
He's their man, on a roaming tariff with a PTS, Insane army.
Never heard of 'A Brave New World' Invited in to defend it!
For 35 years No one mentions Dimona, Israel's Nuclear Arms
Development. '1973 ready to drop 30 nuclear bombs on Egypt
Yet denounce any other country's rights to blow up Our World.
'Might is Right' Is what we've got, it's all Irrational Madness!
'Yo Someone's gotta blow up the North Koreans and Iranians'
Threats to our Civilisation, the Planet, they've produced WMD.
Who is the biggest Manufacturer of Armaments in the Cosmos?
Poisoned gases, New Technologies coming ashore with Thor!
*

'CANNOT LIVE IN FEAR'
Putting the whole World into a frenzy.
Excuses to bring out that Program!
"I guess money is a beautiful thing"
We're so easily hypnotized,
"Say cheese!" (& in Mandarin!)
"No Time to go Green ~ go Nuclear!" (Solar cream) Bang!!
We're all to blame, everyone's weak, what did you expect?
For something full of fantasy, 'Welcome to Shanghai Disney!'
Everyone a fashionista wants to live there, if you're Allowed.
City of the Future, moving without noise.
Learnt that in Prison!
*

'Climate Change'
Mother Earth
Is in heat
*

'Watch the Gap'
Trapped in a red hot Vagina ~
'As you like it' ~ A Lovely smile.
Shiva Meditation makes Mind redundant......

89

Absolutely Tao
Everything you said ~ "is all synchronicity"
The Green & blue planet's Indigo Kindergarten.
Feels like I'm in a bubbling spaceship
Dream timers at the Mardi Gras.
Her perfect beam * rushing particle accelerators
~ In our pumping hearts.
An oracle of desire expressing seduction by a crackling fire.
Attached to these thoughts, passing through the head,
being enslaved * Alive Not Dead
*
Tibet is ¼ of China!
Himalaya Glaciers ~ 1/6 of World's Ice (source of water, life)
for now ~ Lake Manoswara feeding six Major river systems!
Highest fresh water lake in the World ~ to 2 billion people!
Himalayan Plateau has its own Inland sea ~ 'Qinghai lake'
The Magical Properties of Land; Sweet attachment.
Shamanic ~ belief, communication with Spirits.
Mantra reverberations throughout the Universe
through 5 elements; Earth, Air Fire, Water, Space.
Magical landscapes, natural forces, being here ~
30 million years of tectonic plates moving
Inside 'Qolomango'
'Mother of the World'
Buddhist horns sounding in the valleys ~
A Spiritual engine deep in the Monastery.
Escaping from the Suffering Cycle ~
'Activities benefitting all beings Model'
Giving the 'Spiritual Consciousness'
needed to go through the Ignorance ~
Tuning into the Intuitional cellular vibe.
Lamas have no fears of tears.
Spirit ~ Death is Not Death

Life is Sweet
Fair as a yellow lotus; Nestled in her 'mons veneris
'I'm here for You & You're here for me'
Do what the fuck you like Venus
Ideas manifested; Free to be ~ fun, chaos
somebody's controlling our space shuttle, Eros.
Be the Best you can as a human being be ~
I could see it and wanted it, Understand!
"It's not a John Wayne movie thing!"
Woke up surrounded by jasmine hair.
Coming up from Underneath.
We are free spirits ~

*

Have to be more conscious, subtle than that!
Zyklon B. Killing gas; How do you spell 'Diablo' Machiavelli,
Pinochet, Kissinger? Understanding the FEAR arising in you.
"Get back in the box, before we put the hood and chains on!"
"It's how humans will evolve, feeling karmic Resistances!"
"You're not here to just eat, drink, sleep, fuck & be fucked!
On your feet slave" ~ "Let's Go Mad!"

*

'In transit'
"Are You a traveller ~
Intruder or an Invader?"

*

Seeing Varuna in a Clear Night sky
A field of Consciousness
Religion A Spiritual Manipulation
fields of dreams
fields of attachments
fields of addictions
fields of distortion
Space of blissful nothingness

Caesar with a Pirated Noble Peace Prize!

No it was 'Majestik' the Interface between the MIC. and ET's.
Not Insane; recovery from 'Operation MK Ultra & Paperclip'
Surely you must realise from the false 9/11 reports, WMD'S;
The Illegal Invasion and War in Iraq, the Bank bailouts; that
people are being abused in a Police State, you have No rights.
Who's ready to Stop the Dark Fascist Forces making disaster!
All the contradictions now Visible, it must make you Wake Up!
Illusionist manifesting a Statue of Liberty in Quantanamo Bay
Which country has a passport with the Devil on the cover ~
and imprinted on the forehead with a 3ʳᵈ Reich eagle flying?
Mass Manipulation of the guilt of another Holocaust; Try Yale.
You've got to know 'bout Skull & Bones & the Federal Reserve.
Who's got the Monopoly in the Opium Market today pardner?
He supplied all the Coke to Washington in his Executive Jet!
Sold out his gimp character to Mephisto in a machismo latex suit.
If you have Integrity you're their biggest enemy; Screwing you!
Took a shot in the back of the head; The Matrix is eating itself.
It's getting less dense as we go into a new DNA Soul dimension.
Every experience we have is a Treasure can be lovely Pleasure.
Now we have to face ourselves ~ If you have RESONANCE
If you accept the character then you have INTEGRITY
Otherwise 'Welcome to the FEAR & HOPELESS DESPAIR'
How much can you TRUST TRUST TRUST TRUST ~
Won't have any problems dropping the emotional body
below the navel, chakras keeping us connected to the EARTH.

*

System's Quality Control!

Seen so much shit in Fort Detriek, Maryland. Antibody process.
It's a Vaccine that's going to kill you, fuckin' your Immune Sys.
"It's a letter from the Devil, c/o the holy Trilateral Commission"
Kiss of death from a Psycho pikey in a furry bikini with a spear.

This Time Form
'Yoga is discipline ~ Tantric is Integration'
Given the Crystals to spread out
Helping the process unfold ~
The Lineage of blue
The Knowingness ~ transmutation
Wisdom in the Heart

*

Crystal * You Own It
'The language of a Magic bullet'
Opening your eyes to see ~ Allowing the flower to unfold.
This Awareness you will have if you give it to yourself.
Hard sell when you have to be believable.
"Pitch 'em high, look 'em in the eye, watch them buy"
I'll have to let go of the body, the new experience in Allowance
of the moment to moment. Creating being ~ in the happening.
Giving yourself the way ~ You are the way!
Choosing from a Menu of the Flower of Life.

*

Overloaded nerves
"Hey you fall in Love in India"
Always getting the Love Card.
Maybe I'll get a Lakshmi cookie.
Allowing Yourself to fall in this Consciousness
Not putting your Ego in the way
Still the Free Will
of Discerning where you want to go ~
Depends on your Blockages, resistances!
Seeing the World out of a Psychic's drama.
Stress in your body ~ until you come to Peace
Allowing it to go through ~ a space to see it.
This is natural Stimulation & this is Simulation!
Living you have a choice ~ Acting upon it

'Cupere' Sunbed

Party Yoga, Fruit Salad Yoga, Trance Yoga, Tantra Love Yoga,
Work Yoga, Decorating Yoga, Pain Yoga, Hot laughter Yoga,
Breakfast Yoga, beach Yoga, Psychedelic Yoga, Yoni, lingham Yoga.
Up at dawn ~ Don't forget you're still alive!
Constant reinvention of Energy ~ Do something New
Right here right now
No Going back > new strings new chapter.
It has to work its Magic
Healing space & time ~
Light left the body ~ Spirit feeling in the heart.
Life in you will continue ~ Supernovas, new Suns being born

*

'The Heroin Tan'

Myths of ascending Kinder eggs "I love the rush of a chillum!"
Keep Smoking! If that's the flow why let it go? Very minimal
Sweet & Petite ~ She's got that sticky and smelly stuff ~
Is it Shakti day? You begin to learn India has lots of secrets.
Whatever I'm getting I'm enjoying. She's got the same texture!
"She might come" ~ "I love her so much!" ~ "Please come"

*

Intense Voice

I trust in the moment ~ You're Allowing yourself the Experience.
I'm the Gift; Take it or leave it; I'm the tool of this happening.
You see yourself as in a relation/ship ~ on a different plane.
Don't put me in the tumult ~ Turning Point.
If you combine Mind & Heart ~ You go in the Knowing.
"Words combined with Love become a Poem"

*

Rudraksh Beads

"I like my brain chemistry now ~
Armed to the teeth with drug experience.
Goddess of the Universe ~ throbbing Full Hearts

In response to the images of the G20 conference
Demonstrations in the City of London on 1st, 2nd April 2009.
In particular the 'death' by 'Internal bleeding' of Mr. Tomlinson
who would have been an anonymous casualty probably put
down to 'natural causes' It certainly seems that the Official
reaction was that and no Police officer came forward with any
statement to refute this. It was only when video film was later
shown from an Independent observer who filmed the incident
with eye witness corroboration that Mr. Tomlinson in fact was
heavily pushed to the floor with a metal baton struck against
his legs. What affects me is the typical 'Cover up'/'Spin' from
the Military style authorities, the lies and therefore corruption.
Having lived in Goa in March 2008 when Scarlett Keeling was
allegedly raped and murdered with a police, political cover up
I condemned their corruption and compared it to the honesty of
British Police. My naiveté is apparent now. What sickens me is
not only the 'Hype' by the Media/Police to Criminalize all these
protesters who have legitimate rights in a democracy to Protest
but also the fact that Mr. Tomlinson was trying to go home after
working and had nothing to do with the G20 Protest. He's seen
innocently passing the Police with No 'Anti social' attitude or
provocation to any Violence in fact he has his back to the line
of police who are in full riot gear And he had his hands in his
pockets so offering no direct threat to them! He was brutally
struck to the ground and two minutes later died of Internal
bleeding whilst on the ground not one of the Police Officers
went to help him up! To me what is most worrying about
the incident is this Authoritarian Force behaving as a gang
of goons described in the days of the fascist/Gestapo of Pre
-WW2, Nazi Germany especially with the fearful scene of
German Alsatian dogs on the leashes of the City of London
Police surrounding this sole innocent human being! 'Police
Unaccountability and the Public's lack of trust must change!'

To the Outer Limits (Violence in every tribal bible)

'Vatican strangling you all, an Inquisition stretching your Mind!
On a screeching rack; Holy Blood stains all over the sacrificial
ground. Controlling the Psychology of Society through Myths!
Keepers of the Fraud of Faith, blasphemers, heretics, crusaders.
The Heartlands of International Conspiracies and Terrorist Acts.
Who Extracted the False Confessions from whom, in the Media!
Who Planted the Pancake 'Evidence' with Absolutely No Proof?
No Interception from the Cardinals in white Thermite hoodies
Technically Impossible "Is this Real World or an Exercise?"
Who's in charge of mobilizing the War Games? 'Oh mein Got!'
Seeing our brothers & sisters jumping through the dust clouds!
Brainwashing, another whitewash by an 'Imperial Commission'
Globalised Evil, Hypnotising you with WMD; Slogans of deceit.
Who's the new Enemy you Created to make a Patriotic Society?
Wind them up with revenge! Need $100 billion to equip an Army,
need new rules engaging a rampant Military Industrial Complex.
Access: Economic, Scientific, Political, Religious, Legal, Media.
Inside job 'Subversion not election' Making human beings Mad.
Cause ~ Reactions, Who Wields The Power? Who holds the debt?
Who are the slaves who are the slave owners? Central Banksters
had banks collapse in Nations Controlled by mega credit/bonus.
Superstate of Bankers, Economic Crisis, Inflation, Interest Rates,
Money supply, bankruptcies, Debt, loans, Credit swindles, TAX!
"Panics are Scientifically created, Increasing the Money supply"
Which Monopoly caused a Recession, a World wide depression?
Legal Tender backed up by what? Nothing! War a Control Tool.
The Federal Reserve Ultimately Controlling Society, the World!
What happened to an abysmal standard of very poor regulators?
How a democratic government allowed this to happen to people!
Who is getting ripped off, who's making a fortune, who allows it?
Needs a new paradigm, life inspiration ~ www.livingthefield.com

Spinning Untruth Order

'We need $Trillion from the Federal Reserve to fight for Right!
For WWl; The Great depression 1929, WW2; The Korean War,
The never ending Cold Wars, the Vietnam War, The Guerilla
Wars happening all over our Global Empire, Iraq War1 and 2,
Afghanistan Invasion, Israel attacking Iran, Nuclear weapons!'
A need to borrow more Debt from Private International banks.
A few Oligarchs make massive Profit on Interest in these deals.
Who is influencing these foreign policies for War, conflict and
Economic Crisis; Who's deciding who will be our next enemy?
Who uses surrogate states to do their dirty work, who's making
catalysts, pretexts like WMD, terrorism, undemocratic regimes;
Protecting Strategic resources for their own 'National Interest'
Inciting ideological aggressors in Wars as pawns of their own.
A 'Big game' ~ for One Centre of Power!

*

Wake Up Time! Behaving Worse than your Enemy!

'Getting rid of the Constitution for Our Home Land Security!'
What happened to your Civil liberties and to prisoners' of war
being Tortured; Others 'Extraordinarily Rendered' for Torture
abroad how criminal, how diabolical is that for the leader of the
Democratic free world, to be a respected role model? In flames!
Dividing & Conquering, killing themselves, last man standing!
'Manufacturing of War and who Manufactured your Education?
Think tanks, 'Psychological Operations Command' know exactly
which buttons to click to get the required results. They can even
go publicly in front of the Security Council and boldly Lie to the
World and Create a War of Devastation for Millions of People!
How is Your Conscience General, are you eagerly anticipating
meeting the Prince of Darkness Mr. Secretary of State, are you
ready for Your trip to Hell Mr. President & Mr. Prime Minister?

*

(Arrangement Inspired by www.thezeitgeistmovement.com)

Who Cares!
More Compassion ~ let's be Realistic!
Turn your cheek, being detached.
Let him do it as he's in a mess.
Drop the fears that's the trick
The Miracle of Waking Up.
Profiting from Projecting your Pain.
Infected Jewel

*

Lost In the Image
Not making that box around.
No more Judgment of what you do ~
But how you do it! What are you Projecting?
'Share & Care' ~ Doing it with lots of Joy.
This Contentment ~ of being fulfilled
Not the Suffering; If you don't want.
Your free choice ~ behaviour
She was Really ~ A butterfly

*

Changing Connections
Love Yourself More
To Open Up ~
Don't Betray Yourself
Mass Crisis ~ Be Yourself
Always ~ Yes & no flow
trust trust trust trust trust
from the Heart (not the nuts).
Where you get your guts ~
(Power) to dump your Soul mate!
Celebrate life with him, her, it flux
Coming from the Core
Get on with life ~ And not the denial
Your free will to leave

In The Heart
Tears of Unconditional Love
Being in the Oneness
of who you are ~
*

Vipassana
You have to Celebrate Life ~
Give it to Divine Cosmic nature
or too much ego existing.
The Compassionate waves
The Clarity of Mind
*

When your Consciousness goes Up and Up ~
Throw all the bad thoughts away, when you have no Fear
have less resistances, blockages;
When you are not Scared
to be in Love ~
What to do?
Keep your Purity.
*

Aventurine Mathura
Alive Water ~ reflections
A lot more Crystals and Peace
You create your own Reality.
We live what we create ~
Dosed it! Getting High on H2O.
Through Vibrations of Pure Ma Ganga!
'The Power of Amethyst thought' in flow ~ Feeling.
London's reflection ~ Intention of its water's molecules.
We manifest life in our streets, what we think ~ & drink.
A Plastic bottle's dead water ~ lost its Live Prana!
Clear Rose quartz water will cure that disease!
Your Mind is Free

The Biosphere ~ 30 million other species being in It ~
Which King are you Listening to?
Looking death in the Face
with a smile in your heart.
Did you work for a clear conscious
Did you forgive the unforgivable
Did you live for Love in Life
Did you worship the gift of being
Did you feel the Unconditional Love of Children
Did you sacrifice all for the truth
Did you plant the flowers of Peace
Did you create the perception of transcendence
Did you grow the seeds of a spirit
Into blossom
*

On Call
The same High class gonorrhea! "Ay Caramba!"
Organized Crime ~ Obrigado, la Policia.
"We all have our dreams of happiness"
"They need to stop the Armored Personnel carriers
coming into Impoverished areas"
Because we are human & we carry on achieving ~
Let's have an equal distribution of Resources (finite)
"You'll pay in ways only Jesus knows about"
If you break the Law of Real men!
A favourite favella Gangster chic.
Girls on the street feeding their families.
Fugitives with knives on the beach
Kalashnikovs & testerone in the samba,
no rhymes or reasons. Survive to eat.
A factory making wraps from bricks of cocaine.
Fun & games in a Rio blackout.
"Watch out for snipers' bullets!"
Where the lead is heavy.

Shadows going into the Darkness
'Concept of a Prison of Chains' & attached to a cross!
'The Emotional Field' "What's wrong with you?"
Your Experience… "I felt so Guilty!"
Make it Peace ~ It's All in Tune.
"I never knew what a swear word was until
I went to Confession when I was six."

*

Full Nuclear Disarmament!
The Deliria of my Poetic Imagination.
"What's in your heart?"
Our Interchangeable Highest Ideals ~
Embracing all around ~ no desire to harm
Man ~ Nature as one

*

Communicating in the Emotional Field
Where's Victoria Vetri of 'When Dinosaurs Ruled The Earth'
when you really need her? Liberate all scary, guilty, shameful
demons in the shadows. "Where Am I?" Recreate feeling it all.
Don't need any happy pills; Face up to the reality ~ Feels Real
Understanding the Processes, of pain, hate, desire, greed, loss.
Don't need to be a Victim or to cause another human disaster!
Blaming others, sinking to the depths running from the Truth.
Negative thoughts and actions living in your body and Mind.
What do you want to put in your Space? Free Spirit or a slave?
Allow it all to be Consciously, subtly and gasping delightfully.
Your Suffering can become your teacher, learning to let it flow
Getting to know 'Maya' falling for Ignorance ~ being in trance.
Finding your unique gift

*

Philosophy
If you like it ~
it's good for you

Psychedelic Yoga
"Are You Sunshine?"
"I think you're my Sunshine"
"It ain't hard gettin' 'em, it's getting' rid of 'em!"
'Having a good idea without thinking of anyone else!'

*

Koans in Union
Whistling Messages from Outer Space.
"Feed the Hungry" ~ "Stop the Killing"
"Let there be Light"

*

Rio Babylon
There is this life force thing
There is the spirit thing ~
Best to look after the immune system.
Starts with a Bang and an incident!
What triggered the seeming accident?
What was there to cause the Bang?
Potentiality of Pythagorean Ignition.
Ask questions into unknown territory.
Is nature a coincidence or is it not
Is something higher ~ Synchrony Socrates?
Resurrection of an esoteric living planet.
Getting voices, music from the spheres
Choosing the right frequencies
Meditating on Eve breathing

*

Pagan Child
'The Mind Creates the Universe with a thought'
Aspiration Inspiration, battles of Power & Respect.
Life in itself is Perfect; Suffering is a concept ~
Crucified on a Cross for all to see, to Fear being Free!
Honoring they serve your Spirit ~ not leaning down on you

To Anicca ~ Anicca ~ Anicca
Please don't miss isles ~
Silver porpoise, pastel flying fish.
Calmly watching each Instant
Changing ~ Buddha sky.
True Happiness, Taking the liner 'Meditation'
waves surf ~ the Sea of Moments
a new beginning

*

Antibodies
Drop the curse, stress, nerves, delusional pain, disorder.
Mass manipulator – no need to stand on your head
or batter a frail, local pensioner to eat their daily bread.
Belligerent system, toxins in the body, digesting shame.
Throw it up to the wind, don't blame me.

*

Pill Box
The Grim Reaper's rat a tat tat, horrible Death & Destruction!
Terrorised beyond your Imagination or dancing in Exstasis ~
'With molecules of bliss ~ Something must Exist'
Radio Active rocks, X Ray, Uranium, Alpha particles, Radium.
Found sub atomic atoms in all the Oceans of the World.
Why so much Empty space? Had a leap of energetic genius.
Making hay with nymphs while the sun shines.
Came back, Creative flow ~ Can't Stop

*

Psychedelic Hieroglyphics
"You bring sublime meaning to the non sense of speech."
Celestial Crystal Space ~ beyond ~ the conscious Mind
Integration with your own natural subconscious flow of Life.
'Come to Goa and give up ~ sweet surrender'
"I'm completely Open ~ to you"
Peace, Love not War
'Beautiful' ~ What a Smile!

ABOUT SUNNY JETSUN

*Inspired by the sixties Sunny started traveling the world in 1970.
His spiritual journey on the hippie trail to India took him through
San Francisco, Los Angeles, London, Amsterdam, Paris, Vancouver,
Sidney and Kathmandu to Varanasi. His arrival on the sub-continent
was the beginning of writing autobiographical verses capturing his travel
experiences, encounters with remarkable people and his quest for self-
realization. Combining experimentation with drugs, sex, rock & roll,
meditation, Love and life in general. Sunny started to open up to a multi-
dimensional Universe. He lived the mantra, "Turn on, tune in, drop out"
realising Mind's-illusions, inspired by deeper feelings of holistic nature,
empathy*energy & Space.*

*Over four decades Sunny has written and published 28 books of poetry,
created over one hundred paintings, traveled the World and considers
his masterpiece to be his daughter. He has spent the past fifteen years
in Goa, India inspired by the freedom to experience and idealism of
human consciousness.*

Sunny Jetsun books and art are available on the web at:

*Website: www.sunnyjetsun.com
Facebook: www.facebook.com/sunnyjetsun
Amazon: www.amazon.com/author/sunnyjetsun
Smashwords: www.smashwords.com/profile/view/sunnyjetsun*